An Introduction to
Program Evaluation

An Introduction to Program Evaluation

JACK L. FRANKLIN   **JEAN H. THRASHER**

A WILEY-INTERSCIENCE PUBLICATION

JOHN WILEY & SONS, New York • London • Sydney • Toronto

Copyright © 1976 by John Wiley & Sons, Inc.

All rights reserved. Published simultaneously in Canada.

Reproduction or translation of any part of this work beyond
that permitted by Sections 107 or 108 of the 1976 United States
Copyright Act without the permission of the copyright owner
is unlawful. Requests for permission or further information
should be addressed to the Permissions Department, John
Wiley & Sons, Inc.

Library of Congress Cataloging in Publication Data:

Franklin, Jack L.   1931–
   An introduction to program evaluation.

   "A Wiley-Interscience publication."
   Bibliography: p.
   Includes index.
   1. Evaluation research (Social action programs.)
I. Thrasher, Jean H., 1934–   joint author.   II. Title.

H62.F694   309.2'12   76-4789
ISBN 0-471-27519-0

Printed in the United States of America

10 9 8 7 6 5 4 3

Preface

The emergence of program evaluation as a management subspecialty is only the latest in many attempts to improve administration through the application of those principles and methods of science that have so revolutionized the industrial and technological spheres of the society. Most such attempts have had little lasting impact, although administration has emerged as a separate discipline in some areas. Innovations such as those incorporated into "scientific management" had little influence in the administration of public programs, however, because most managers of public programs are trained in disciplines in which management is not considered an essential part of their curricula. Program evaluation is considered to have a more promising future than most such experiments because its emergence and development has been a resultant of economics more than of scientism.

The demand for program evaluation increased so rapidly that when managers and evaluators began their collaboration they were poorly equipped to optimize the contribution of each. Evaluators, drawn largely from research-oriented disciplines, lacked awareness of the managers' priorities and constraints. Managers, drawn largely from service-oriented disciplines, found the language, the statistics, and the demands of evaluators baffling and inconclusive. There are signs that the situation is changing. Service-oriented disciplines are including management courses in their curricula, and research-oriented disciplines are beginning to include courses in evaluation in their curricula.

This book is intended to be a textbook for neophyte evaluators and practitioners as well as a reference book and source book for operating program managers and program evaluators. It is designed to be appropriate either as a text or as supplemental reading in courses on program evaluation; research methods; applied research; public administration; health, mental health, and public health administration; social work administration; applied social science, rehabilitation, and others designed to train managers or program evaluators. It is also intended to assist the managers and evaluators of social programs to understand better the needs of the other so that the full promise of program evaluation can be realized.

We take the position that program evaluation is possible and is a valuable organizational activity. We discuss program evaluation as a process from the organizational, managerial, and research perspectives and indicate areas of difficulty, accomplishment, and promise.

We thankfully acknowledge our debt to Mr. David Stephens and Dr. Lee Kittredge for their critical and editorial suggestions and to Mrs. Peggy Wilkerson for her assistance in preparing the manuscript.

JACK L. FRANKLIN

North Carolina Department of
Human Resources
Raleigh, North Carolina
January 1976

JEAN H. THRASHER

North Carolina Division of
Mental Health Services
Raleigh, North Carolina
January 1976

Contents

Evaluation, Program Evaluation, Evaluative
Research • Continuous versus One-Shot
Evaluation • "Hip-Pocket" and Formal
Evaluation • Policy Research • Applied
Research • Decision-Oriented Research • Social Audits • Action Research • Operations Research • Discipline-Related Research • Basic Research • "Front-Line" Evaluation •
Utilization Review • Continuous Monitoring • Quality Control

Theory • Selecting a Model • Selecting a
Design • Experimental Designs • Quasi-

An Introduction to
Program Evaluation

1
Introduction

In an era of heightened public concern about the distribution and management of public funds, at a time of diminished buying power, when an ideology of a "good return on an investment" competes with more charitable and affluent ideologies for ascendancy in the public ethos, evaluation becomes a prominent and visible concern for the managers of public programs. Program evaluation, although certainly a popular term in current management vocabularies, is not a new activity and historically has emerged and developed along with administration as an independent specialty. Most writers agree, however, that program evaluation as a specialized function is largely a post-World War II emergence, so its history is necessarily brief [1]. The purpose here is not to trace the historical

1

development of program evaluation, but rather to indicate that the recent and current emphasis, and in a strange way the popularity of program evaluation, and its emergence as a developing speciality both within management and certain academic disciplines, is a response to a particular set of circumstances.

In a democracy ultimate accountability is to the public; the public, by direct expression and through its elected representatives, is increasingly demanding a rendering of that account, particularly in the case of social programs. No longer is the provision of a service sufficient justification for its continued support, as has been the case for education for most of our history and for health care for the past 40 years. No longer is there consensus about "the American dream" and "the good life" to provide a rationale and justification for public programs designed to reach this dream or actualize this life. (Consensus never existed, but policymakers acted as if it did, so the result was the same.)

The universal cure for a program adjudged to be ineffective has been the increased injection of resources, particularly money, into the program. Now the public and legislators are asking for a demonstration of the soundness of program concepts. The public has continued to grant, as a general rule, that "it is better to be rich and healthy than poor and sick," and policymakers have continued, with surprisingly few exceptions, to point to the excellence of training, devotion to cause, and dedicated hard labor of the managers and professionals who operate most public programs. But both are asking, "So what?"; not "Is it worthwhile?" but "Does it work?" Confronted with these questions, managers have had to look beyond their traditional advisory specialities and seek another kind of specialist, the program evaluator.

One direction managers looked was to the private sector, particularly to business. It made sense. After all, evaluation had been an integral part of most business enterprises for some time, and in addition to lawyers, the legislative and policymaking bodies of this country are comprised of more businessmen than anyone else. Businessmen often have even less modesty than lawyers about the range of their abilities. From business came systems analysts, management analysts, and cost accountants, each armed with techniques tried, and sometimes proved, in the world of private enterprise. The transition from business to public programs was not an easy one, however, because most of the criteria of success—higher profits, greater production, increased sales, lower costs, and so on—are not immediately applicable in most public programs, where the "product" is people and not things [2], and where the objectives, although rarely explicitly stated, are certainly *not* manufacture, sales, nor monetary profits. Attempts to gear evaluation to the aspects of a program that could be measured, or at least recorded and documented, gave rise to the often justified complaint from practitioners that they were being evaluated on the least important of their activities and their insistence upon the essential "intangibleness" of their accomplishments.

Another direction in which managers looked was academia. This, too, made sense. After all, what managers needed were data, and who could doubt the power of research to provide answers to difficult questions or the contribution of researchers to Western technology. That the consequences of research were often new problems for new research has never been a serious brake to the acceleration of applied science, and the social sciences were assuring each other, and trying to convince everyone else, of the ability of science, properly applied, to direct the deliberations of problem-solvers from the lowest to the highest circles. Although program evaluation, like most "applied" fields, occupied the status of a second-class citizen within institutions of higher learning and such attention as it received was in the nature of controversy over the "ownership" of program evaluation by one or another carefully delimited discipline, managers were both democratic and ecumenical about the whole thing and accepted equally economists, political scientists, sociologists, statisticians, psychologists, and just about anyone else who volunteered or could be lured. These persons brought with them an unblemished ignorance concerning the "real-world" decisions managers must make, the daily demands made upon them, and the nature of unideal organizations operating in untypical ways. They brought with them also, however, an undaunted assurance in the correctness of their methodologies and the power of their techniques.

What managers contributed at this point was their experience and a real and growing sense of problem. They had been making evaluations all along—evaluations about what worked and what did not, the best course of action, the optimal allocation of scarce resources, and so on. The correctness of these and future decisions now required documentation, and different skills were needed to augment the managerial armamentarium and to aid in policy decisions, a situation which, when recognized, aroused widely varying combinations of relief and resentment.

If, in the early days of the emergence of program evaluation as a specialized function in public programs, it could be called either a science or an art, it was closer to the latter, and the boldest colors were those painted by the brushes of faith and frustration. While the whole enterprise was goaded by necessity and sustained by faith, frustration became a major topic of conversation—at least in the published literature. The list of these frustrations was, and is, legion: Learned treatises were written on why evaluation is impossible; behavioral scientists complained that they could not "control variables" because programs were changed in the middle of their research so that they were always in the position of evaluating what no longer existed; managers complained that they could not wait upon the privileged leisure of research; analysts and accountants complained of poor bookkeeping and cost controls; and clinicians complained of added paperwork and the questioning, implied or real, of the adequacy and accuracy of their professional judgments. All of these arose in addition to those issues that everyone agreed were issues—program survival, the need for adequate comparisons, the attribution of causality, and so on. Other problems, which involved the organizational politics of program evaluation, included the status of evaluators within an organization; the locus of control of evaluation; the use of evaluation, veto power, sponsorship, and so on. Nearly all of these sources of frustration continue to exist, with varying degrees of intensity and varying degrees of legitimacy. Some of the disputes arise with the incorporation of any new specialty into an ongoing system. Most, however, result from an unwillingness to adapt either methods to programs or programs to methods and an unshakable faith on the part of all parties that a solution exists, valid, if not for all times, at least for all situations at a given time.

To try to describe the present "state of the art" in evaluation is hazardous at best because it is a discipline in constant flux. Evaluators are accepting the limitations of their abilities and have faced the fact that their activities must be geared to the information needs of multiple audiences. The evaluation and information needs of practitioners, clinicians, managers, and policymakers are quite different, and evaluators are increasingly willing to compromise the rigor of their accepted techniques and to recognize the limited utility of their findings. The result has been less "scientific," but more immediately useful, evaluations. Managers, who acknowledge the need for evaluation, have come to accept the fact that evaluation is neither a magical process, nor an immediate panacea, nor the ultimate threat and that meaningful evaluation requires some accommodation by the programs. Examples of the total integration of planning, implementation, and evaluation are rare, however; where they do exist, they are most often on the level of service delivery rather than program effectiveness.

At times evaluators still are greeted with an affection usually reserved for auditors and inspectors general, but their utility is increasingly recognized, especially as managers attempt to justify their programs to funding sources and explain themselves to other groups. A number of evaluation techniques have by now had their effectiveness, if not the scope of their applicability, demonstrated. The fact that evaluators now talk about "the state of the art" is itself an encouraging note, implying that the positive assurances with which many evaluators initially addressed their tasks and the high expectations with which they were greeted have been moderated by cold confrontations with reality and that all parties concerned are getting on with the task of developing the necessary tools and conditions to realize the high promise of the discipline. Most of this volume is an explication of the "state of the art" and is aimed at correcting a deficiency by contributing to the adequate and realistic preparation of evaluators.

In retrospect, the emergence of program evaluation as a management specialty has certain elements of slapstick comedy, but the importance of that emergence, the form and function program evaluation assumes, is a very serious and important concern. If evaluation is to influence managers and policymakers to base judgments and decisions on other than experience or expediency, certainly evaluation must be superior to these alternatives. More than for any other emerging specialty within the social and behavioral sciences, the quality and utility of evaluation require immediate verification. Circumstances do not permit a long incubation period, much less an adolescence. Evaluation is a multidisciplinary endeavor, and few evaluators have multidisciplinary training. While there are many examples of hybrid disciplines (Culture and Personality is a recent case in point) program evaluation must mature much more quickly because it is *basically and essentially not an academic discipline*. The future of program evaluation is immediate, and although the problems are many, the prognosis is good. One purpose of this book is to enumerate some of the elements that comprise program evaluation and to indicate their utility. The essentially utilitarian rather than academic nature of program evaluation is what provides it with considerable power. This same factor also imposes unusual strictures of quality because the potential harm from poor or improperly applied evaluation is much more immediate and the consequences more costly in terms of money, human effort, and service delivery than in most academically based social and behavioral disciplines. There is probably no universally applicable answer to the question of whether no evaluation is better than bad evaluation, and in the abstract it is not a productive argument; but in any given situation no evaluation at all still remains an alternative to be seriously considered. Some examples are presented in this volume.

Attempts have been made to bring order and synthesis to the diversity of approaches and definitions which have characterized the field of program evaluation. One of the earliest, and certainly one that has had considerable impact, was the work of Suchman [1:60–73]. Elaborating on the earlier work of James [3], Suchman constructed a typology that combined the dimensions of locus and sophistication and distinguished five types of evaluation: effort, performance, adequacy of performance, efficiency, and process. Some writers, including Etzioni [4], have criticized this typology for omitting certain important categories, such as organizational analysis. Others have felt that the typology is overinclusive, focusing on inputs that may be outside the proper realm of evaluation [5] and encroach upon areas traditionally claimed by clinical research.* Some of these concerns are discussed in Chapter 2, but it is enough to

---

* In many ways this is an unfair criticism, because Suchman specifically states, "Strictly speaking, however, analyses of the processes whereby a program produces the results it does, it not an inherent part of evaluative research"[1:66]. These authors contend that under certain circumstances such concerns are within the legitimate purview of program evaluation.

point out here that such discussions have had the laudable result of making program evaluators more self-conscious about the legitimate scope of their enterprise—much to the relief of everyone.

A related development, largely independent of program evaluation but warmly embraced by program evaluators, has been the various attempts to adapt the advances in computer technology to be viable tools for human service agencies. These attempts have run the gamut from simple record storage, through systems simulation, to the programming of computers to conduct clinical interviews. Of particular interest to evaluators have been attempts to use computers in the development of management information systems, large-scale data banks, and simulation models.

The unwillingness to accommodate either programs or methodologies to the demands of the other has been, and continues to be, a real problem. In a sense, however, the argument that this problem generates is spurious. Without question, in a situation that is, for whatever reason, inflexible, the evaluator must adapt his methodology to the demands of the program—with whatever cooperation he can muster. Programs do change to accommodate evaluation, especially programs which have built-in evaluation mechanisms. Usually, however, the evaluator is there to assess the program; the program does not exist to provide the evaluator with a research laboratory. This brings into focus one of the crying needs of program evaluation: the need for innovative and integrative methodologies, models, the techniques that are explicitly designed to handle the practical realities of ongoing programs. Historically, such methodological breakthroughs have come from the research centers—in modern times, the universities. The universities have not been particularly responsive, although the trends are changing and exceptions exist. This places a double burden on the evaluator—the need to be inventive and responsive and at the same time to maximize quality and utility. To meet these needs, his methodological equipment would require the addition of the following innovations:

1. *A reasonably inexpensive accurate epidemiology.* The demand for estimates of need for services, particularly the extent and distribution of undesirable or problem conditions, is increasing. This is crucial in areas such as mental health and services for the aged where the need for services is difficult to determine and the right to service unestablished. Epidemiological studies, however, are both expensive and time-consuming. Instruments do exist, of course, some coming from the massive attempts at health epidemiology, but there is no degree of professional consensus about the adequacy or proper application of the studies or the instruments developed for and out of them. The Health Opinion Survey (HOS) [6–8] can serve as an example of many currently available epidemiological tools. The format of the HOS is an easily administered checklist of symptoms often associated with mental illness. The respondents are asked to indicate the frequency with which these symptoms are experienced. A composite or average score for a population is then used as a comparison point for gauging the relative mental health of that population. The HOS is unlike most such instruments because it has been widely used and normative standards have been established. In common with other similar tools, however, is

the difficulty in interpreting the HOS, especially in populations with large subgroups and the temptation to use the HOS as a diagnostic instead of epidemiologic tool. Epidemiology remains a luxury few programs can afford. Other approaches, such as social area analysis (in urban areas) and extrapolation from existing surveys (e.g., alcoholism) are often appropriate compromises, but they remain only compromises when epidemiology is required.

Estimates of need are closely associated with the evaluation schemes and management systems discussed in Chapter 3 and are discussed in more detail in Chapter 5. Many evaluation schemes and most management systems require clearly stated goals and unambiguous measures of goal attainment. In the past goals, if stated at all, were in terms of services to be delivered, man-hours to be expended, costs, and other factors directed toward the program itself. The increasing demand for accountability— questions of "So what?" and "What difference does it make?"—resulted in the present emphasis on goals stated in terms of impacts on some target population (units such as individuals, families, groups) in need of the services offered by the program. Before impacts can be determined, the target population must be defined. But the demand for techniques of estimating the size and characteristics of the population in need of services far exceeds the supply, and some uneasy compromises have been made. For example, one model for estimating mental health needs [9] is based on the assumption of an overall 2 percent level of illness in the general population. Using available census information, the 2 percent is further divided into appropriate percentages of age, sex, occupation, race, and so forth, giving specific estimates of the number of persons in need of mental health services. These estimates are then compared with the number of persons who actually received care, and the differences are the unmet needs of the target population.

Making such prevalence estimates requires platonic reasoning and the application of metaphysical assumptions. For example, if there are a known number of people in the general population with certain characteristics like those of the people served by a program, causal relationships between these characteristics and the *problem* addressed by the program are most often unknown. And even if the characteristics were known to have an important causal relationship, the fact remains that most individuals in the target population are not served by the program. All of the characteristics derived by planners, managers, and consultants to describe a target population "in need" of the program services may fit many individuals who do not need, want, or require the services of the program to overcome the "problem" or to continue to function with the "problem" [8, 10].

2. *Criteria for success and ways to measure it.* Most public social programs are essentially qualitative in nature—that is, the changes that they attempt to bring about either in people (health, welfare, education, employment) or in their environments (environmental protection, public housing) are usually changes in some quality, often at some future point in time. The evaluation of such programs, almost without exception, is addressed with methodologies that are equipped to deal with quantities. The quantitative evaluation of qualitative programs has been a dilemma for some time. However, program managers have made some progress toward compromise—that is, they have made

some effort to quantify their goals and aspirations, and evaluators have attempted to "qualify" their methods to accommodate the aspects of programs that presently defy quantification. The evaluation of programs whose primary emphasis is prevention so mismatches available methodology and program needs that few have had the courage to attempt it.

One of the most promising approaches to creating a fit among the needs of program managers and evaluators is that of goal achievement, which has many variants (see Chapter 3). This approach has the advantage of using the client as his/her own control and of making evaluation measurable and relevant to the client's problems. Disadvantages, for both implementation and evaluation include the difficulty some professionals have making goals for clients explicit, the cost, the need for clinical judgment (for which most evaluators are not qualified), and the fact that often the success of a program is *not* the same as the sum of successes of individual clients. Nevertheless, it remains a promising approach to the problem. The major difficulty, however, is that how well programs can be adapted to this or any similar model is limited, and new models and methods are required to deal with qualitative aspects (which, again, are often the most important) of social service programs.

3. *Cost-benefit analysis.* In the future cost-benefit analysis may well prove to be the most powerful evaluation tool. Managers must weigh the cost of programs against the expected benefits. This is particularly true when choices must be made among programs or when there are alternative proposals for new programs. *Effectiveness* is a more common term, but the term *cost-benefit analysis* more

clearly specifies the dimensions of the problem. Cost analysis techniques have been well developed in business and industry and can be adapted to social programs without undue difficulty or prohibitive expense. The delineation of a unit of benefit, however, has remained elusive and probably depends upon the definitions of success alluded to above. The major problem, however, is that most human conditions are relative and are best conceptualized as continua. There are many degrees of health, affluence, quality of life, productivity, and any other condition defined as desirable or undesirable. While obtaining agreement about progression or retrogression is often possible, defining these directions in terms of *units* (i.e., one, two, or more degrees or steps of better or worse) has not yet been possible.

4. *A realistic model of organizations.* Evaluators' knowledge of organizations comes from one or more of four sources.

Experience, which is probably still the best but is not, by itself, sufficient.

A study of organizational theory, which, despite its long history, rests on two basic models, both of the genre ideal-typical—the structural model and the human relations model. Attempts have been made to synthesize these organizational models, but they remain fairly discrete basic assumptions about organizations and how they work [11, 12].

General systems theory, which is based on the assumption that organizations have certain characteristics in common by virtue of the fact that they are systems, which is true, but which ignores the fact that they are systems manned not by parts but by very fallible people. A

systems approach has the additional drawback of including the assumption that a knowledge of particular organizations is sufficient to know the precise relationship
between particular organizational parts and particular
program outcomes.

A psychological model, in which an organization is seen
as the sum total of the personalities of its interacting
members. A person's behavior in an organization is
assumed, correctly, to be a function of that person's
psychological makeup and experience, but the fact that
behavior in an organization is also shaped by ·a person's
position within the organization, the nature of the information channels, and other characteristics of the organization itself is ignored.

5. *Controls.*   The question of controls in evaluation is
vital. The outcomes of services may be measurable, but
judging these outcomes against those of alternative services
or no service at all is not always possible. Control groups, in
the classical sense, are usually not feasible in public service
programs because of high cost, ethical concerns, and time
constraints. Random assignments of services is also rarely
possible because of the presumed specificity of program to
problem and the ethical problems inherent in the withholding of service. As in other areas, some approximate solutions have been used, but new techniques and methods
are needed to solve the very real problem of controls.

6. *The evaluation of preventive activities.*   Except for a
few diseases with very specific characteristics or programs
whose goals are the fairly quick elimination of a condition
(mass immunizations, for example), the evaluation of prevention (activities such as education and consultation) has
remained a methodological headache. Stated simply, the

problem is one of determining what would have happened if an activity had not taken place, or if some other activity had taken place. The measurement of nonevents is a realm that science has been happy to leave to the writers of fiction. Attempts have been made, of course, but these have had to rely largely upon the expectations and satisfactions of the participants. [13, 14]

7. *A new multivariate model.*   One of the major complaints of program evaluators is that programs do not "hold still" for evaluation. Programs have always been changed based on the informed hunches of their administrators, inspired insight, changes in legislation, political expediency, or political edict. Few programs have been changed on the basis of program evaluation. There is no reason to believe this situation will change substantially in the near future, nor is there much pragmatic justification for such a change. The situation facing the evaluator is, simplified, this: He has the capability of measuring outcomes and changes but lacks the ability to ascertain causality for these changes; he is capable of researching program processes but cannot "control" these processes and must usually operate in the absence of consensual standards of adequate performance; he has the ability to measure inputs or efforts but is powerless to control alterations in these inputs.

The ultimate solution is not to gain greater "control" over these widely fluctuating variables so that they better approximate the demands of existing models, preferably the model of the controlled experiment; what is needed are new models that can "accommodate" the vagaries of real-life situations. Sometimes, of course, the circumstances are not so bleak. On occasion, the commitment to evaluation is sufficient to hold programs more or less intact for the evaluator and even allow a certain amount or randomization. Large-scale social experiments, such as public housing and the guaranteed income, are examples. On a smaller scale, Goal Attainment Scaling [15–16] has been successfully demonstrated in part because of its allowance for compromise in addition to its relatively limited scope and relatively generous resources. Programs that are frankly experimental have frequently been able to incorporate evaluation in their design but usually lack comparative standards. The task of devising adequate multivariate models makes the task of putting a man on the moon seem simplicity itself, but then, if the limit of man's ingenuity has been reached, man has yet to admit it.

These are but a few of the many problems in program evaluation that call for new models, techniques, and methodologies. They are not presented in a spirit of negativism nor to imply hopelessness nor to cast doubt upon the worth of evaluation. Nor are they presented as a prelude to offered solutions, as much as we would like to be able to do so. They are given merely to present as full a picture of the state of the art as possible. The state of the art at this time is probably not so confused as these pages make it seem. That evaluators often have to address problems that are too big with resources that are too few is a problem that an individual evaluator must confront in a particular situation, but the fact that evaluators must attack these problems with a patchwork quilt of methodology is an approachable problem.

The book is intended to serve as an introduction to program evaluation, a textbook for those who are contemplating entering the field, and as a guide for managers who are concerned with what to expect from evaluation and how to use it. We begin by exploring the scope and types of evaluation and how evaluation is similar to and different from other types of activity. From there, we describe some of the prevailing methodologies, their uses and contraindications. The problems and pitfalls of evaluation, examples of different types of evaluation, and sources and types of evaluation demands and resources are discussed. We end with some prognostication about the future of evaluation as an emerging specialty and a management tool.

Most of the illustrative material in this book is taken from the area of mental health, reflecting the professional concerns and experience of the authors. The issues addressed and the techniques discussed, however, are equally applicable to the fields of public health, education, social welfare, developmental disabilities, public administration, nutrition, gerontology, rehabilitation, poverty, delinquency, criminal justice, and many others.

REFERENCES

1. Edward Suchman, *Evaluative Research,* Russell Sage Foundation, New York, 1967.
2. Harvey A. Garn and Mancur Olson, "Human Services on the Assembly Line," *Evaluation,* I(2), 36–42 (1973).
3. George James, "Evaluation and Planning of Health Programs," *Administration of Community Health Services,* International City Managers Association, Chicago, 1961, 125–218.
4. Amitai Etzioni, "Two Approaches to Organizational Analysis: A Critique and a Suggestion," *Administrative Science Quarterly,* V, 257–278, (September 1960).
5. Joseph S. Wholey et al., *Federal Evaluation Policy,* Washington, D.C., The Urban Institute, 1970.
6. Dorthea C. Leighton et al., *The Character of Danger,* Basic Books, New York, 1963.

7. A. M. Macmillan, "The Health Opinion Survey Techniques for Estimating Prevalence of Psychoneurotic and Related Types of Disorder in Communities," Monograph Supplement #7, *Psychological Report,* III, 325–339, (September 1957).

8. Michel Lousignant and Guy Denis, "Psychiatric Patients and the 'Untreated' Cases of Epidemiological Surveys: A comparative Analysis of the Self-Concept," *Social Science and Medicine,* IX, 39–42, (1975).

9. Beatrice M. Rosen, *A Model for Estimating Mental Health Needs Using 1970 Census Socioeconomic Data,* National Institute of Mental Health, Series C, #9.

10. Bruce P. Dohrenwend and Barbara S. Dohrenwend, *Social Status and Psychological Disorder,* Wiley, New York, 1969.

11. Daniel J. Levinson and Eugene Gallagher, *Patienthood in the Mental Hospital,* Houghton Mifflin, Boston, 1964.

12. Jean H. Thrasher and Harvey L. Smith, "Interactional Contexts of Psychiatric Patients: Social Roles and Organizational Implications, *Psychiatry,* XXVII, 389–398, (November 1964).

13. George B. Hutchinson, "Evaluation of Preventive Services," *Journal of Chronic Diseases,* XI, 497–508, (May 1960).

14. Fortune Mannins and M. F. Shore, *Consultation Research in Mental Health and Related Fields,* Public Health Monograph #79, Public Health Service Publication #2122, U.S. Department of Health, Education and Welfare, U.S. Government Printing Office, 1971.

15. Thomas J. Kiresuk, "Goal Attainment Scaling at a County Mental Health Service," *Evaluation,* Special Monograph #1, 12–18.

16. Thomas J. Kiresuk, "Goal Attainment Scaling: A General Method for Evaluating Comprehensive Community Mental Health Programs," *Community Mental Health Journal,* IV, 443–453, (1968).

2

What Is Program Evaluation?

Program evaluation shares with most emerging specialties an overabundance of definitions and a paucity of consensus. To say that there are as many definitions as there are evaluators is not too far from accurate. Despite the absence of agreement, an "evaluator" is reasonably able, within the constraints of managers, to define his field, and thus his role, fairly freely. As a consequence, definitions of program evaluation tend to have a strong flavor of the disciplinary backgrounds of the definers. Conversely, because a certain amount of prestige is attached to program evaluation, there is a tendency for those with other related responsibilities to define their roles to include evaluation.

Thus, there is a "territorial" issue both among those who claim to be evaluators and between those who claim "evaluation" functions, and both issues are independent of the definitions of managers, which are often even more idiosyncratic. Many major publications simply bypass the issue of definition and assume some sort of secret convenant between author and reader. The situation, however, is not really chaotic, and fluidity is to be preferred over premature closure; certainly it is to be preferred over a preoccupation with definition. The importance of having definitions is not so much to achieve consensus as an end in itself but stems from the fact that the way evaluation is defined influences how evaluation is utilized, and thus, how it is conducted.

Among the narrower definitions of program evaluation are those that limit the focus of evaluation to outcomes. One of those who takes this position is James Ciarlo, who more for technological than ideological reasons, states: "The focus is limited to *outputs*—and *only* those outputs which are related to the achievement of program objectives" [1:1]. Furthermore, outcome or impact evaluation is limited to "what those services actually do to and for the people who receive them" [2:1].

Only those who hold an ever narrower view and who admit economy as the sole evaluative criterion exclude program outcomes from the legitimate realm of program evaluation. Most writers, however, take a somewhat broader perspective than Ciarlo. Many evaluators follow the lead of Suchman [3] and broaden somewhat the definition of impact to include the analysis of effort (program inputs) as well as outcome. They explicitly exclude any consideration of program activities (process evaluation), considering this to be the proper domain of the administrative or clinical sciences.

A broader definition, and one that does incorporate some program elements, is that recently suggested by the Southern Regional Conference on Mental Health Statistics: "determining the degree to which a program is meeting its objectives, the problems it is encountering and the side effects it is creating [4:75]." This definition does incorporate some of the concerns of business and accounting; the authors go on to state that "it [program evaluation] involves monitoring of several factors simultaneously—funds, personnel, client intake, problems, quality of services, outcomes" [4:75]. Because of the arrangement of the Southern Regional Conference volume, it is difficult to know what the authors specifically exclude by this definition, but presumably organizational analysis, needs assessment, and certain other activities sometimes considered as program evaluation are not included.

At the other most inclusive end of the continuum of definitions are those illustrated by Binner, who concludes: "Hence we should reserve the name 'program evaluation' for when we are referring to a comprehensive evaluation of the entire system under consideration and call it 'problem or procedure evaluation' when we refer to some segment within that system" [5:10]. By "comprehensive evaluation" Binner refers to determining the value and cost of each juncture of the treatment process from entrance to exit, indirect services, alternative services, and the impact and contribution of the larger social contexts [5:1–10]. Binner is advocating a systems approach to program evaluation and, if taken literally, would leave very little outside the legitimate concern of the evaluator.

The position taken in this volume is a reasonably broad one and includes within the boundaries of evaluation the process of securing valid, reliable, and applicable information about programs, program structures, processes, outcomes and impacts, to permit managers to make decisions for program improvement and fulfill their responsibilities for public accountability. There is some advantage to maintaining a focus upon outcome or impact in any definition of evaluation, but with a recognition that a thorough understanding of program outcomes requires the integration of information not itself specifically addressed to outcomes or impacts. Thus, for the purposes of this volume, program evaluation is defined as the determination and assessment of the results (outcomes/impacts) of program activities. Any number of management strategies become program evaluation when and to the extent that they contribute to the improved assessment of program outcomes. Activities that are commonly called effort evaluation, process evaluation, quality control, and so on might or might not be program evaluation, depending upon the intent or use. Some of these distinctions are further clarified in other parts of this chapter. These and other activities are valuable management tools in their own right, but become program evalution only when and to the extent that they contribute to an understanding of program outcomes and the factors that contribute to or hinder those outcomes and the efficiency of their accomplishment. This definition combines elements of previously quoted definitions by placing the emphasis of program evaluation upon outcomes, but noting that the evaluator must be prepared to engage in a wide variety of other activities to make the analysis of outcome a viable contribution to management.

EVALUATION, PROGRAM EVALUATION, EVALUATIVE RESEARCH. The terms, *evaluation, program evaluation,* and *evaluative research* actually refer to quite different aspects of the same phenomenon, or more specifically, each is a special instance of the term preceding it. *Evaluation* is by far the most global and inclusive of the three terms, denoting, as it does, the determination of value or worth. Evaluation is an element in nearly all managerial decisions as well as all other decisions. Another common use of the term *evaluation,* particularly in social and health programs, is the assessment of needs or eligibility of individuals or families for services—as in diagnostic evaluation, developmental evaluation, rehabilitation evaluation, social services evaluation, and so on. This use of the term *evaluation* does *not* make any judgment concerning the value or worth of the individuals being evaluated but only their problems and eligibility. Evaluation, when the term is applied to programs, is not related to this use of the term and is concerned with individuals only in the aggregate.

Program evaluation is a particular type of evaluation. As the name implies, it is concerned with the "value" of particular programs or program elements. Various definitions have already been presented that reflect different opinions as to what should be the scope of program evaluation, the proper model of program evaluation, or the proper role of program evaluators. It is a rather broader term than evaluative research because many types of program evaluation do not require the rigors of scientific research, and many situations requiring program evaluation do not permit such rigors and their associated investments of time and other resources. Most of this chapter is concerned with program evaluation, and the term* is defined further by example and comparison.

The distinction between evaluation and *evaluative research* is most succinctly summarized by Suchman:

> In our approach, we will make a distinction between "evaluation" and "evaluative research." The former will be used in a general way as referring to the social process of making judgments of worth. This process is basic to almost all forms of social behavior, whether that of a single individual or a complex organization. While it implies some logical or rational basis for making such judgments, it does not require any systematic procedures for marshaling and presenting objective evidence to support the judgment. Thus, we retain the term "evaluation" in its more common-sense usage as referring to the general process of assessment or appraisal of value.
>
> "Evaluative research," on the other hand, will be restricted to the utilization of scientific research methods and techniques for the purpose of making an evaluation. In this sense, "evaluative" becomes an adjective specifying a type of research. The major emphasis is upon the noun "research," and evaluative research refers to those procedures for collecting and analyzing data which increase the possibility for "proving" rather than "asserting" the worth of some social activity. [3:7–8]

What this quotation clearly indicates is that *evaluative research is a particular type of program evaluation* and is the

---

* The term *program*, as used here, refers to an interrelated set of activities designed to accomplish a common goal. It does not, therefore, refer to any particular level of activity.

method of choice when possible and appropriate. It is essentially the application of scientific methods to management decision-making about the worth or productivity of programs. The specific application of some of these scientific techniques are discussed in the next chapter.

CONTINUOUS VERSUS ONE-SHOT EVALUATION. If administrators consider evaluation to be one of their central responsibilities, they are apt to believe that evaluation should be a constant and continuous process. In practice, this has led to an emphasis upon input and process evaluation (see Chapter 5). In social programs the development of statistical systems—often quite sophisticated—and standardized tests are the most notable examples. Statistical systems reflect a desire and a need on the part of managers to know something about the clients being served by their programs and something, in an aggregated way, about what happens to these clients and how staff members spend their time. When such systems are reasonably well developed, they provide fairly detailed information about the demographic characteristics of clients, at least some indication of how clients happen to enter the program (e.g., source of referral), at least a categorical assignment of why the client entered the program (e.g., diagnosis), how staff time is expended among various types of activity (work/time analysis), and often what should be the next steps (disposition). Less often, but still with laudable frequency, such systems also provide information tracking the client through a system or program—services provided, transfers, and so on. Typically, a statistical system provides some of these types of information, depending upon the preferences of managers and the availability of resources, and statistical systems are probably the best developed and most widely used form of continuous evaluation in social programs. Continuous evaluation focusing upon outcome is deplorably rare and probably is most closely approximated in the field of vocational rehabilitation, where evaluators are able to report on the numbers of persons rehabilitated, their earning power, and so on.

The use of standardized tests as a tool of program evaluation is probably most fully developed in the field of education. Such tests are used widely in programs in which a choice can be made about who enters the program, and average scores on such tests are often a source of great pride or challenge to some institutions and programs. The same tests that provide criteria for entrance into some programs provide a source of pride or chagrin to those managing the programs from which persons "are graduated"; thus, to a limited degree, they are used as outcome measures. Except in public schools, standardized tests are seldom used in programs which cannot choose their entrants. The difficulty is not that they are not available, although criticism is directed at all extant tests and their use, but rather the high cost of such tests or their limited utility for decision-making. Continuous evaluation that incorporates outcomes and impact is the ideal, and only if there is continuous evaluation can evaluation be fully incorporated as a management function.

One-shot evaluation is more apt to be a response to a perceived crisis, a particularly difficult policy decision, or possibly, the receiving of a grant. Typically, evaluative research is "one-shot" in nature, because it usually involves "a study." For whatever the reason, one-shot evaluation is aimed at answering a specific question about a particular program or program element at one point in time. The sources of crises are legion but usually result in the immediate need for information about a particular aspect of a program. There is a strong tendency, usually out of concern for credibility (see Chapter 5), to use outside evaluators in crisis situations, although what constitutes "outside" depends upon the organizational level of the crisis. Consultants are often used in just such cases, and management consultant firms have multiplied in large part as a response to the frequency of such crises.

Policy decisions require a different kind of "one-shot" evaluation. Usually such decisions require a choice among several means of reaching the same ends, and so raise questions of effectiveness and cost. Policy decisions are more likely than crisis situations to require in-house evaluations; like crisis situations, they are likely to impose tight time limitations. Almost without exception, the policy decision involves some sort of comparative evaluation—one technique against another, two or more techniques against a standard (either developed or inferred), or relative cost. Usually, although not always, the concern is with expected results.

The awarding of grants, contracts, or special funds is usually associated with innovative approaches and is aimed at testing more than at problem solving or implementation. Most of the research-oriented mechanisms of evaluation were initiated as special projects, although often for purposes other than program evaluation. Evaluators have been able to adapt the efforts of numerous others to their own needs because of the catholic qualities of research and the real-world qualities of program evaluation.

Periodic evaluation is a very useful midpoint between one-shot and continuous evaluation. Although many social phenomena change rapidly (e.g., public opinion and military situations), most do not. The changes wrought by many social programs are often slow in developing, or at least the impact is slow in emerging. This is particularly true for education and prevention programs. In addition, many of the instruments available for measuring change are sensitive only to gross changes. In many instances, particularly those requiring measurement of impact, long-term outcome, or prevention, neither continuous evaluation nor one-shot evaluation is adequate, but some type of periodic monitoring is possible, feasible, and necessary. Periodic evaluation permits some rest to the evaluator while he deals with other problems, and at the same time it does not compromise his, or the program's ability to grow.

"HIP-POCKET" AND FORMAL EVALUATION. "Hip-pocket" is considered a somewhat polite euphemism for "the seat of one's pants" and is sometimes even further glorified as "evaluation by expert judgment"—when the expert is also the manager. Program managers engage in "hip-pocket" evaluations many times a day. In one sense, every managerial decision is a "hip-pocket" evaluation.

On occasion, the "hip-pocket" evaluation is the responsibility of the evaluator. He is, in this circumstance, acting more in the role of consultant or expert than in the role of researcher or management subspecialist. Evaluators frequently fail to perform in this role. Whether the evaluator comes from a background in social science or business, he is usually accustomed to approaching any task armed with facts, figures, and other information which are applied to the situation. If they fit, fine; if they do not, tough. Situations in which the evaluator must not only "diagnose" the problem but also "prescribe" for it, without time for prior preparation and often without time for adequate reflection, are uncomfortable. The evaluator must depend upon his knowledge and experience, just like the manager. His potential value lies in the fact that the evaluator's knowledge and experience are apt to be different from those of the manager and so ideally can complement the manager's skills and decision-making ability.

In its broadest sense, "hip-pocket" evaluation can be defined as the information-utilization which goes into a management decision. It is so continuous and routine that it is seldom graced with the name *evaluation*.

Formal evaluation could be described as any specified activity that bears the title *evaluation,* were it not for the fact that the current visibility of evaluation has resulted in many activities designated as evaluation would more properly be regarded as basic research, applied research, discipline-related research, training, or some other field. (See below for discussion of some of these other activities.) In part, these misdesignations are attempts to achieve legitimacy, secure funding, or simply to control the direction of evaluation; in part, they reflect a genuine confusion about what evaluation legitimately encompasses.

For the purposes of this discussion, formal evaluation is considered to be any of a number of activities whose primary and immediate purpose is to inform program managers and decision makers about the state of their programs, the results of their efforts, and the needs for new or changed programs. This volume is almost exclusively about formal evaluation.

The relation of the evaluator to the manager is different in formal evaluation than in in hip-pocket evaluation. Working in cooperation with or at the direction of a manager or decision maker, the evaluator nevertheless works independently, applying his skills when appropriate and providing the manager or decision maker with the results of his efforts. The evaluator is solely responsible for the accuracy, adequacy, and utility of formal evaluations and must be prepared to accept accountability in these areas. The initiation and utilization of evaluation, however, remains the responsibility of the manager or the decision maker, because formal evaluation is but one component of a management or policy decision.

A number of activities closely resemble program evaluation. Some have figured heavily in the emergence of program evaluation; many are an integral part of the professional socialization of evaluators and managers who utilize evaluation. For reasons of necessity, convenience, interest, or expertise evaluators may engage in these other activities, but strictly speaking, only partially or only sometimes are they program evaluation. They do, however, help to highlight the proper scope and domain of program evaluation.

POLICY RESEARCH. Policy research differs from program evaluation in two important ways. First, it is rarely initiated by program managers but rather by directorates or legislatures. Second, it is usually aimed not at gauging effectiveness of current programs, but at delineating new directions. It is similar to evaluation in that it often results from some perceived inadequacy in current directions and programs. The identification of program vacuums also causes policy research to be initiated and precedes any concern for evaluation.

Policy research may take many forms. A common one is the assessment of need, often an activity engaged in by evaluators, but the objective of policy research is different. Major legislation covering the plight of migrant workers, the development of a community college system, the community mental health centers, aid to the aged and infirm, and public housing started with policy research. The purpose was not evaluation; it was to *do something.*

Policy research may be employed in the correction of known or suspected abuses or the prevention of such abuses. The staffs of the many regulatory agencies set up by government bodies at all levels are concerned mainly with policy research—the popular acceptance of proposed policies or the ability of already existing policies to bring about desired results. A third type of policy research is largely legalistic, and is not always considered to be an appropriate application of policy analysis. People who propose laws and those who oppose the proposals all try to amass data to support a particular point of view.

Policy research overlaps with program evaluation in that it involves an attempts to estimate the need for services, to isolate gross inefficiencies, and to suggest remedies. It differs from program evaluation in that it is stimulated by the perceived absence, abuse, or inability of programs. Program evaluation is aimed at the assessment of the adequacy, efficiency, and impact of existent programs, given the policies in effect at the time.

Policy analysis and program evaluation share a common designation as applied social science disciplines, and many of the same methods are used in both. Both are designed to have an impact upon decisions. Their major differences are in their temporal sequence (policy analysis typically precedes program implementation and therefore program evaluation) and in the level of decision making it attempts to influence. [6,7]

APPLIED RESEARCH. *Applied research* is probably the most generic term considered in this discussion. The basic question facing the applied researcher is: "How can we do it better?" (the traditional problem of building a better mousetrap). Applied research had its origins in business, particularly in product design and consumer response, and spread from there to other fields, those usually dominated by basic research. Evaluative research is one kind of applied research, but program evaluation research and applied research have evolved differently. Applied research is usually directed toward the development of new or improved technologies; program evaluation at the need, use, application, and effectiveness of existing technologies and program modalities. Except in the instance of product design (not a major concern of social programs), applied research is nearly always of the "one-shot" variety and, in fact, may not involve an ongoing program at all but may rely upon simulated situations in laboratories or with computers. Program evaluation, however, can never be divorced from actual programs. Whereas applied research is usually aimed at product improvement, program evaluation is usually concerned with program improvement. In short, applied research includes evaluative research as well as many kinds of research that are not related to program evaluation; program evaluation also includes evaluative research but also many activities which cannot be defined as applied research.

DECISION-ORIENTED RESEARCH. Decision-oriented research is one legitimate use of program evaluation and one of the precursors of program evaluation. The only improper use of program evaluation in the name of decision-oriented research occurs when the decision has already been made. Chatterjee [8] gives a tongue-in-cheek but uncomfortably close-to-home account of a fictitious research group which undertakes to evaluate various forms of imposing the death penalty. Elaborate formulae are developed, but the major variable seems to be the support of the legislature. The basic tenet of the research group is never to question the decision of a funding source but rather to assist in strengthening and enforcing a decision already made.

There are many uses of decision-oriented research. Lobbyists, for example, use decision-oriented research to support a predetermined point of view; others use decision-oriented research in a true evaluative sense. Following chapters deal in some detail with the use and misuse of evaluations, but the area of decision-oriented research is one for which the evaluator must often make a "go/no go" decision—and live with the consequences. Both program evaluation and policy analysis are forms of decision-oriented research.

SOCIAL AUDITS. Social audits may be seen as a special case of process evaluation and of quality control. Essentially, social audits, as they apply to social programs, are addressed to the existence and prevalence of programs or program elements. The two situations in which social audits coincide with program evaluation occur when social audits result in the development of social indicators, thus becoming a tool for impact evaluation, and when social audits are used in conjunction with known and established standards, thus making them useful for comparative evaluations, especially when they are tied to program accomplishments or outcome. Perhaps the closest association of social audits and evaluation is in the determination of need for services, which some critics would maintain is not a legitimate activity for evaluators but which provides information evaluators need. In fact, social audits and input evaluation tend to overlap in that social audits are difficult to interpret in the absence of an estimate of need, and estimates of need do not inform managers if the availability of services is not known. Although there are situations of overlap, social audits can at best inform only a small part of the total evaluation responsibility. Social audits are of great importance in program planning. Because good program planning facilitates evaluation, social audits are important to evaluators; participation by evaluators in social audits may therefore have substantial payoffs in the long run. A social audit is one example of an activity which sometimes is program evaluation and sometimes is not program evaluation depending upon the purposes for which it is undertaken and the use to which it is put.

ACTION RESEARCH. *Action research* is a term used synonymously with policy research, decision-oriented research, applied research, or some combination of the three. Sometimes action research is used to assess the effects of certain activities, therefore becoming a type of evaluation; but as a term, it is usually used as a contrast to basic research. One aspect of action research that does not pertain directly to evaluation is the assessment of what steps are necessary to effect a change of direction or implementation of new programs. In this regard it is akin to policy research but is more apt to be focused upon public readiness, public acceptance, sources of resistance, and so on. Market research is a good example of action research; public opinion polls, although not themselves action research, are sometimes used as such or give rise to action research. Evaluation may also initiate action research, but action research almost never initiates evaluation.

Another use of the term *action research* is to distinguish the use of social action programs as intentional experiments from the more tightly controlled small-scale experiments typically associated with social psychology. In this context action research becomes a type of evaluation [9].

OPERATIONS RESEARCH. Advocates of operations research like to think of it as a separate and discrete science [10]. Starting in World War II as an application of science and mathematics to the problems of the coordination of military operations and adopted enthusiastically by industry, operations research has found a number of supporters within nonindustrial organizations. It is a tool for managerial problem solving involving systems analysis and the construction of models, often quite ingenious ones. Operations research is useful primarily with the "physical" problems of management (as opposed to the "human" problems) and, as Halpert and others [11] have noted, has not been of great use in evaluation because most programs lack criterion measures of effectiveness, an essential requirement for operations research. Operations research remains potentially useful as an evaluation tool, however, and is one derivation of the systems model (see Chapter 3).

DISCIPLINE-RELATED RESEARCH. As the name implies, *discipline-related research* refers to forms and foci of research endeavor that are usually associated with one or another academic discipline and for which a particular researcher is specifically trained. Discipline-related research may be either basic or applied, and it can be easily described as biological, chemical, psychological, sociological, pharmacological, or pertaining to some other discipline. Because of the multidisciplinary nature of program evaluation and because of the different intents of basic, applied, and evaluative research, discipline-related research is only occasionally immediately relevant to program evaluation. Discipline-related research is almost always designed to allow the researcher, at the end of his efforts, to make some generalization about the object of his research or about the phenomenon under study. Generalization might be permitted in evaluative research, but the primary concern is the program under investigation, with no regard to whether the program is typical. In evaluative research the same techniques are often utilized as in other types of research, but it always differs from discipline-related research in that evaluative research is initiated by the felt need of managers and policy makers, whereas discipline-related research arises from some problem deriving from within the discipline. One additional difference, only subtly different from the others, is that evaluation research must be of some immediate utility to the program or managers who have responsibility for the program at some organizational level. Discipline-related research has no such restraint.

In recent years there has been some confusion, or at least some blurring of distinctions between evaluative research and discipline-related research, especially involving the social science disciplines. The recent curtailment of federal research funds, which more or less coincided with the more generous funding of evaluation, the greater visibility of evaluation, and its emerging respectability has resulted in a tendency for researchers to propose discipline-related research but to call it evaluation [12]. Some federal agencies have abetted this tendency, unwittingly, by applying the standards of basic research to evaluative research and by a failure to recognize the differences between evaluation and discipline-related research.

BASIC RESEARCH. Stated most simply, basic research is aimed at the generation of new knowledge, and evaluative research is aimed at assessing the results of the application of knowledge. This statement vastly oversimplifies the actual state of affairs, because evaluative research can generate new knowledge and basic research findings are occasionally immediately applicable. The *motives* for engaging in basic and evaluative research are different, however, and these differences are accurately summarized in the first sentence. The basic researcher is only secondarily interested in the applicability or usefulness of his work beyond discovery—the interest of the applied researcher. Similarly, the evaluative researcher is primarily concerned with how knowledge is applied and with what results; only secondarily concerned with contributing to the store of human knowledge. The point to be stressed is that basic and evaluative research do not differ in their methods, techniques, or rigors—only in their intent. All of the distinctions between basic research and applied research found in the literature and among scientists can be applied to basic research and evaluative research.

"FRONT-LINE" EVALUATION. Front-line evaluation differs from the activities discussed so far in that it does not involve a research activity. It is a term, used mostly in the vernacular, to refer to evaluative decisions made at the point of service delivery. It is usually, although not necessarily, based on the subjective judgment of a manager, and the term *front-line* is a clear and intentional analogy to "combat warfare," with all that implies for speedy and flexible managerial decision making. Consultants are ocasionally used in this capacity by managers, but it is usually a type of evaluation thrust upon managers in the absence of more precise information. It is also frequently glorified, however, in the same way that "front-line" officers are compared to their counterparts in noncombat areas. The use of the term serves to draw attention away from the quality of the evaluation or decision and onto the conditions (again with a combat analogy) under which it was done.

UTILIZATION REVIEW. A term originating in medicine, most particularly in hospital medicine, *utilization review* is often associated with accreditation and is aimed at the protection of the patient. It is a process of reviewing practices within an institution or a program to ensure that such practices are in keeping with generally accepted procedures or established standards. Such reviews are intended to guard the patient against either abuse or neglect on the assumption that the patient is not qualified to judge such things for himself. Utilization reviews are concerned with the use of unusual or experimental procedures, the failure to use established procedures, the adequacy of patient records, the length of time a person is kept in a program, the training of those giving services, safety, licensure, and a myriad of other things. Utilization reviews may take many forms. Two of the most common are "peer reviews," one of the ways by which professions govern themselves; and "review teams," usually from outside, which satisfy the requirements of accrediting, licensing, and funding bodies, as well as superordinate management. Utilization review differs from program evaluation in that it is not concerned with the overall effectiveness of procedures, but only with the appropriateness of their application. It is not concerned with the need for services in the population, but, again, only that those entering programs are treated appropriately. It is one type of quality control and shares with evaluation certain techniques—most notably comparison against a standard. Like some of the other activities discussed in this chapter, utilization review could be incorporated into a program evaluation system if it were tied to program outcomes.

CONTINUOUS MONITORING.   Continuous monitoring encompasses many activities. It is a term denoting process and may or may not imply evaluation. Ongoing evaluation is one form of continuous monitoring, but so are primitive statistical systems which do nothing more than count the number of people entering a program. Utilization review is also considered continuous monitoring. Evaluation may be built into continuous monitoring, as in some information systems, but continuous monitoring may refer to nothing more than good bookkeeping. In its more formal aspect, it is a type of continuous program evaluation and is discussed in Chapter 3 as an emerging approach with considerable potential for evaluation. In short, continuous monitoring is one preferred form of continuous evaluation, but the two terms are not synonymous.

QUALITY CONTROL.   Unlike continuous monitoring, quality control implies *intent* rather than process. Utilization review is one form of quality control. Quality control may be one intent of evaluation and is one reason managers have turned to evaluators. Quality control is just what the term implies—a mechanism for assessing, improving, and maintaining the quality of programs. It is not necessarily evaluative research—the research process is too time-consuming to be used for quality control—but the skills and expertise of the evaluator frequently can be useful to the manager in the exercise of his responsibility to assume quality control.

Quality control is a term that comes to the evaluation of social programs from business,where it is used to designate a lower limit below which a product is considered unsuitable or an upper limit on the number of products that can be defective without sacrificing profits. In social programs it refers to any attempt to assure that the services rendered conform to accepted standards, given limited resources and other constraints.

The information and results of evaluation should be used in quality control. Program evaluation is not synonymous with quality control because it encompasses many considerations in addition to quality control. Stated another way, one frequently assumes that the provision of high-quality services does not guarantee satisfactory outcomes, but satisfactory outcomes are not possible without high-quality services. Therefore, high-quality services are a necessary condition to acceptable levels of accomplishment, and quality control becomes an area of concern for program evaluation.

Establishing similarities to and differences from related activities and concepts is, admittedly, a very indirect method of definition; but it can be instructive.

REFERENCES

1. James A. Ciarlo, "A Performance-Monitoring Approach to Mental Health Program Evaluation," mimeographed (January 1972).
2. James A. Ciarlo et al., "A Multi-Dimensional Outcome Measure for Evaluating Mental Health Programs," mimeographed, no date.

3. Edward Suchman, *Evaluative Research,* Russell Sage Foundation, New York, 1967.

4. Definitions and Classifications Committee, *Definition of Terms in Mental Health, Alcohol Abuse, Drug Abuse, and Mental Retardation,* National Institute of Mental Health: Mental Health Statistics Series #8, 1973.

5. Paul R. Binner, "Some Comments on the Need for a Comprehensive Approach to Program Evaluation," *Systems Approach to Program Evaluation in Mental Health,* Western Interstate Commission for Higher Education, Boulder, Colorado, 1970.

6. Duncan MacRae, Jr., "Policy Analysis as an Applied Social Science Discipline," *Administration and Society,* VI, 363–388 (February 1975).

7. Ian Mitroff and Louis Pondy, "On the Organization of Inquiry: A Comparison of Some Radically Different Approaches to Policy Analysis," *Public Administration Review,* XIX, 471–479 (September/October 1974).

8. Pranab Chatterjee, "Decision Support System: A Case Study in Evaluative Research," *The Journal of Applied Behavioral Science,* XI, 62–74 (#1, 1975).

9. Glen Cain and Robinson Hollister, "Evaluating Manpower Programs for the Disadvantaged," in G. G. Somers and W. D. Wood (eds.), *Cost Benefit Analysis of Manpower Policies,* Industrial Relations Center, Queens University, Kingston, Ontario, 1969.

10. Leslie C. Edie, "The Quality and Maturity of Operations Research," *Operations Research,* XXI, 1024–1029 (September/October, 1973).

11. Harold P. Halpert, William Horvath, and John P. Young, *An Administrators Handbook on the Application of Operations Research to the Management of Mental Health Systems,* U.S. Department of Health, Education and Welfare, Public Health Service Publication #2110.

12. General Accounting Office, *Report to Congress: Need for More Effective Management of Community Mental Health Centers Program,* National Institute of Mental Health, esp. pp. 32–42, August 27, 1974.

3

Evaluation Designs and Methodologies: How To Do Evaluation

If theories that are peculiar to evaluation exist, they come from theories of management rather than from those of social behavior generally. Many of the techniques and tools of program evaluation, however, have been drawn from the scientific armamentarium. Program evaluation, including evaluative research, is a very approximate science. Although there are neither microscopes nor telescopes, there are useful methods that, if properly used, help to avoid errors. The designs and techniques described in this chapter are drawn primarily from various social sciences and have all been used successfully to evaluate programs. They are techniques by which an evaluator can derive summary measures with known strengths and weaknesses. As in any area of inquiry, the method is the means, not the end.

There is no single design or technique suitable for every program evaluation. The selection of appropriate designs and techniques depends upon the accepted definition of evaluation, the purposes of the evaluator, the question or questions to be answered, and the intended uses of the results. In this chapter the advantages and disadvantages of various traditional designs and techniques are discussed, along with some emerging approaches to evaluation.

THEORY. Although there are no theories of evaluation *per se,* most of the programs to be evaluated are outgrowths of established bodies of knowledge. The evaluator must be familiar with this knowledge, with any supporting theoretical constructs, and certainly with the program to be evaluated. However, many administrators (and perhaps many evaluators) often mistakingly assume that anyone with a little common sense and a few empirical facts can provide the correct answer on any subject [1]. This almost *a priori* assessment or evaluation is usually the case with hip-pocket evaluations.

When he can be guided by theory—here defined loosely as statements that summarize relationships between variables (an ordering of facts)—the evaluator's tasks are somewhat less difficult because theories indicate the types of variables that are important. Theories also suggest expected relationships between particular variables, thus aiding in the selection of independent variables and in making decisions about how much change can realistically be expected in the dependent variable.

Few, if any, evaluation studies include discussion of the theory or theories involved in the selection of variables included in the project. They need not include such discussion, but systematic evaluation requires knowledge of theories in the area of concern, even though these may not be explained in a formal report.

SELECTING A MODEL. A model is a part of theory, but more specifically, it is a picture of the program or project to be studied. Programs are usually complex and difficult to describe, and models must be constructed to present programs in simplified form, thus facilitating evaluation by limiting and specifying the variables to be considered.

There are two conventional models used in the evaluation of programs—the goal attainment and the systems model [2]. A goal attainment model contains the intended consequences of the program (official goals) and the processes of the program that are considered to be highly influential in determining the extent to which the program achieves these goals. A systems model takes into account the fact that programs pursue other activities besides those related to the attainment of official goals and that there is frequently competition among official goals for scarce resources. Some of these activities center around maintaining the system and may or may not be related to official goal attainment. In some programs concern for system maintenance activities sets limits on the organizational energy available for the attainment of official goals.

Systems models are divided into two general types—

closed and open—with much discussion devoted to the advantages of the latter. A closed-systems model is based on the assumption that a program exists as an entity and is relatively impervious to outside influences. The variables included in this model are intraprogram variables. For example, if in evaluating the effectiveness of a treatment program in a mental hospital the evaluator uses a closed systems model, the responses of patients to treatment are considered adaptations that depend only on events within the hospital.

In an open-systems model, variables that are "imported" from outside the program are considered in addition to intraprogram variables. Although the open-systems model is widely discussed and praised as being more in accord with real-life situations, the terms *open* and *closed* are relative. Any one evaluation study may involve a host of variables, but closure is necessary at some point. Therefore, one could argue that all evaluation and, indeed, all research ultimately relies upon a closed-systems model. In general, the systems model serves as a map of a program to answer the question: How close does the allocation of resources among program elements approach an optimum distribution [2]?

The evaluation problem suggests the model to be used. If the question concerns the extent to which the program is achieving its goals, the goal attainment model will suffice. If the question is more complex and concerns the optimum distribution of resources among elements of a program, the systems model is perhaps appropriate. We use "perhaps appropriate" because the systems model requires a great deal more knowledge and understanding about program activities and is more expensive than the goal attainment model in terms of effort and money. Given the kinds of information needed to understand a system, the scarcity of techniques for the integration of this information on a systems level, and the costs in time and money, the systems model is impractical for most evaluation. It is, however, an important management perspective, and attempts to apply a systems approach to evaluation are increasing. For the most part, a systems approach is an attempt to relate all aspects of a given system and is particularly promising as a method for anticipating or predicting likely outcomes. Applying engineering and operations research techniques, a systems approach involves systems design, systems simulation, and testing [3].

SELECTING A DESIGN.   In designing the evaluation of a program, the evaluator seeks to determine the effects of an activity, a program, or any other variable of interest and to establish that other factors do not explain these effects. In more technical terms, the evaluator is concerned with a study design with known internal and external validity. Internal validity refers to the extent to which the design allows the effects of a treatment, a program, or any other variable to be accurately determined. The design with high internal validity is thus a tool for precisely answering the question: Did the treatment or program make a difference in this instance? Campbell and Stanley [4] list seven threats to internal validity which, if not controlled by the design, could produce erroneous findings. These are effects of history, maturation, testing, instrumentation, statistical regression, selection and selection-maturation interaction. External validity concerns the extent to which the results of one evaluation can be generalized to other programs in similar settings. For most evaluations, internal validity is far more important than external validity, but in some cases, such as the evaluation of a regional version of a national program, the evaluator ideally strives to maximize both internal and external validity. Because evaluation studies almost always take place in less than ideal situations and trade-offs between the ideal and the possible are the rule rather than the exception, the evaluator designs a study to rule out as many alternative explanations as possible, thereby increasing internal validity.

The basic language of proof is well-controlled experimentation; but most often complete control is either not possible or not practical, and program considerations are almost always primary. For the conscientious evaluator, the choice then becomes one of either designing a study that will best provide answers to questions posed by program personnel, given the constraints mentioned, or of not doing the evaluation.

In this section various designs are discussed—some rigorous and elegant with high internal validity; some that have less internal validity but may be more practical; and some that do not permit valid inferences about program or treatment effects but, nevertheless, may be useful in certain instances.

EXPERIMENTAL DESIGNS.   Classical Controlled Experiment (Pretest-Posttest Control Group Design). In its simplest form the controlled experiment consists of selecting two subsamples at random from the sample population, measuring selected characteristics of both groups, exposing one of these to the program being evaluated and remeasuring the selected characteristics of both. The effect of exposure to the program or treatment is determined by comparing any changes in those exposed (experimental group) with changes in those not exposed (control group.)

This design is diagrammed as follows.*

	Measurements Before	Exposure to Program	Measurements After
Experimental Group	O_1	X	O_2
Control Group	O_3		O_4

Random Assignment

The effect of the program is considered to be the difference between any changes that occur in an experimental group ($O_2 - O_1$) and any that occur in a control group ($O_4 - O_3$). The total effect of a program, the changes in the experimental group which did not appear in the control group, is therefore ($O_2 - O_1$) − ($O_4 - O_3$).

This design is rigorous and elegant when used to determine overall effects of a program (e.g., treatment) because it controls for any change that might occur in the experimental group other than that produced by the program or treatment. The experimental design is also appropriate for assessing effects of program strategies, techniques, and treatment if they can be isolated from others used in the program. The strengths of this design are achieved by ran-

* In research designs an X represents exposure to a program, the effects of which are to be measured. An O refers to both the process of gathering data to measure these effects and to the data gathered.

domization and the use of a control group. Randomization is an essential part of a true experimental design because it prevents systematic differences in the initial status of the experimental and control groups. Matching individuals on certain characteristics (e.g., sex and age) is not a substitute for randomization. However, matching pairs of individuals and randomly assigning one of each pair to the experimental and the other to a control group does increase precision. Randomly assigning individuals to experimental and control groups rules out the possibility that prior differences in individuals could account for the between-group differences appearing after exposure to a program or treatment. Thus by randomly assigning individuals to experimental and control groups, any differences between these two groups observed after the experimental group has been exposed to a program or treatment which were not observed during the 'before measurement' can be attributed to the effects of the program or treatment.

Example 1. The posting of bail has always been a prominent feature of the administration of justice in this country. Its avowed purpose is to ensure that an accused person will appear for trial. Critics of the bail bond system argue that it is unfairly punitive to the poor and often the only exchange of money is between the accused poor and the bail bondsman. To evaluate the effectiveness of the bail bond procedure, judges in Manhattan randomly assigned arraigned persons to one of two groups. Half of the accused persons posted bail in the usual fashion. The other half were released on their own recognizance. The hypothesis was that if the posting of bail is effective insurance that an accused person will appear for trial, more of the first group would appear for trial than the second group. The experiment clearly indicated that bail is not an effective deterrent to judicial elopement [5].

Example 2. To evaluate the effect of a new form of information presentation on managerial decisions, 22 graduate students were randomly assigned to two groups and engaged in simulated decision-making situations. The control group was presented information in standard formats. The experimental group was given the same information in a newly designed statistical summary format. Each group was tested on the quality of decisions, the time to make decisions, and the confidence placed in the decisions. The results showed that those in the experimental group made better decisions but took longer and had less confidence in their decisions than did those in the control group [6].

Example 3. To evaluate the effectiveness of treating schizophrenic patients at home using medications, newly admitted hospital patients who met certain criteria were randomly assigned to one of three groups. Those in the experimental group were treated at home with the help of medications. Those in the first control group were also treated at home but were given placebos. The third group was treated in the hospital. The two home-care groups were tested on a number of dimensions both before and after treatment, and the hospital group was given the same tests after treatment. Thus, both the effects of the treatment setting and of the medications could be examined. Two and a half years later, over three-fourths of the experimental group could be successfully maintained at home. Five years after the experimental program no differences in the social or psychological functioning between the experimental and control groups were found [7–9].

The classical one-factor experimental design is almost always impractical for evaluation designs because usually only the gross effects of an entire program or treatment are determined. This information may be useful to program administrators in making decisions about continuing the program but provides no information about the effects of program elements that could be useful in pointing out possible improvements of a program. The results obtained from this study design are also limited in their applicability because they can be generalized only to identical programs.

Several extensions of the classical one-factor experimental design, such as the Solomon Four-Group Design [10, 4] and Fisher Factorial Designs [11, 4], allow examination of the effects of program elements and increase generalizability of the findings. Other powerful and elegant designs should also be considered by evaluators. However, only in rare instances are evaluators able to exercise the amount of control required by experimental designs; therefore, these designs are not presented here. The interested evaluator is referred to the Campbell and Stanley volume [4].

Experimental designs are praised more than they are used. However appropriate for laboratory use, these designs are seldom used in program evaluation. A number of writers have deplored this fact [12] and some place the responsibility for this dearth upon administrators and evaluators: "Apparently, there is more lack of intent, money and technical resources than of available, applicable methodology. Inflexibility is more in the minds of planners, researchers and critics than in the methodology itself" [13:70].

The picture may not be as bleak as these authors suggest. A recent large-scale review of the mental health evaluation literature (a field in which ethical concerns make randomization very difficult) showed that 15 percent of the studies utilized both control groups and random assignment to treatment and control groups [14].

There are many ethical, political, and administrative reasons why classical experimentation is rare in program evaluation. The most frequently cited reason is that the establishment of randomized control groups (essential to classical designs) frequently means the withholding of services. However, Stanley [13] and Campbell [15] both point out the potential threat of an experimental design to administrators. The design rules out competing explanations and leaves little room for interpretation to the administrator's advantage. In Stanley's words, "the administrator may have no place to hide" [13:67], and evaluations that threaten the status quo tend to be strongly opposed. Much of the frustration concerning appropriate evaluation designs results from evaluators' naive outlook concerning behavior within organizations. Finally, the underuse of experimental designs is due in part to the fact that often they are unnecessary to answer administrators' questions, and providing answers to the posed questions within a mutually agreed upon framework is what most evaluation is all about. Although powerful in producing accurate answers to the question: What impact did the program have? experimental designs are costly, politically sensitive, and often impractical.

QUASI-EXPERIMENTAL DESIGNS. Several well-known quasi-experimental designs do not require random assignment and control groups but, when carefully used, provide reasonably high internal validity. Unlike experiments designed to rule out the effects of influences other than exposures to the program, quasi-experimental designs often depend upon the possibility that these influences can be ruled out by other techniques. In all cases, but especially when using other than experimental designs, the evaluator should examine alternative explanations of any changes attributed to program influences and rule these out.

Time Series Design. The time series design consists of a series of measurements of groups or individuals before exposure to a program and a series of measurements during and after exposure. It is diagrammed as follows.

Measurements Before	Exposure to Program	Measurements After
$O_1 O_2 O_3 O_4 O_5$	X	$O_6 O_7 O_8 O_9 O_{10}$

Postprogram measures are compared with preprogram measures to determine the effect of exposure to the program. This design is rigorous in that it rules out most of the threats to internal validity, but it fails to control for history—that is, time series designs fail to rule out the possibility that something other than program exposure caused any difference between pre- and postprogram measures. Careful attention to other events to which the sample might be exposed aids in determining the legitimacy of ruling out effects of other influences as alternative explanations for any change observed. In essence, the attempt is made to treat the group as its own control.

The required number of preprogram measurements depends on the stability of the traits or events being measured. Simple comparisons of one or two preprogram measurements with one or two postprogram measurements may be influenced by extremes and, therefore, be highly misleading. As a general rule, as many preprogram measurements of evaluation criteria as practical should be obtained. The number of postprogram measurements necessary for evaluation purposes depends on the expected nature of the impact. If the program is expected to have an immediate massive impact, fewer postprogram measurements may suffice.

The usefulness of this design is limited if repeated measurements are made by the interview or questionnaire approach. Repeated reinterviewing of the same persons may sensitize them to the nature of the changes expected and produce effects that are not distinguishable from effects of the program. If, to decrease this possibility, the intervals between reinterviewing are lengthened, ruling out the effects of history becomes more difficult. For example, psychological tests account for much of the data gathered in mental health research. If patients are tested prior to entering a program, retested at the end of the program, and again one year later, one can never be certain which changes resulted from exposure to the program and which from something else.

Time series designs are especially useful in situations in which relevant and adequate criteria are routinely reported, such as in educational programs; however, these designs are not used as often as available data permits. Instability of data, changes in data-gathering instruments, and a lack of technical expertise to undertake the necessary data collection contribute to the underutilization of time series designs. The present emphasis on developing and improving management information systems and the emerging continuous monitoring model promises to provide fertile data bases for time series designs.

Example 4 [16]. A city in South America was facing a grave and growing problem of hospitalizations resulting from complications following abortions induced for nonmedical reasons. As a response to this problem, family planning programs were initiated. For a number of reasons, controls were not possible. To evaluate the impact of the family planning programs, expected hospitalizations were computed by projection of rates prior to the initiation of the program. The "ratio" of observed to expected admissions over a period of time, corrected and adjusted to reflect the characteristics of the service users, was used as an indicator of program effectiveness. Greenberg is careful to point out that one cannot make causal inferences in the scientific sense from these types of observations (except in the negative sense of no impact) but that, nevertheless, such information could be vital to administrators and decision makers, whose need for scientific proof is not compelling.

Nonequivalent Control Group Design (Pretest, Posttest, Control Group Without Random Assignment). Because evaluators are seldom included in the planning stages of new programs, alternatives to randomization have not been fully exploited. This is especially true in the implementation of new programs or where a variety of program elements (all considered equally effective) exists. For example, if a mental health program is intended eventually to serve a multicounty area but initially will serve only one or two counties, the initial service area could be randomly selected from the larger area. The counties initially served become the experimental group; those not yet being served become the control group. This general scheme could be applied to equivalent services, treatments, or other variables of interest. The nonequivalent control group design consists of measuring selected characteristics of two groups, randomly assigning a program to one group, and again measuring the selected characteristics. Any changes that appear in the characteristics of the experimental group that do not appear in the control group are considered to be the results of exposure to the program. The design is diagrammed as follows:

	Measurement Before	Exposure to Program	Measurement After
Experimental group	O_1	X	O_2
Control group	O_3		O_4

Note the similarity between this design and the classical controlled experiment. The only difference is that individuals from the same population are not randomly assigned to the experimental and control groups. The groups are not equated by random assignment, but if they are similar along characteristics of interest and this similarity is verified by preprogram measurements, the nonequivalent control group design has reasonably high internal but low external validity.

In most evaluation studies the evaluator has no control over assigning programs to one group or another. Probably the program and its clients are intact, and the task is to select a control group that is very similar to the experimental group. This is vital if the results of this design are to be credible. As Campbell and Stanley [4] point out, biases resulting from the selection of the control group often make it difficult to rule out other plausible explanations for any changes observed between pre- and postprogram measures. Careful use of this design thus necessitates considering alternative explanations for any changes observed, making these alternative explanations explicit, and estimating their effect on the findings. If these steps are followed, the nonequivalent control group design is a practical reasonably powerful design for evaluation studies.

In an interesting study of the validity of quasi-experimental designs, Deniston and Rosenstock compared two before-after designs without control groups and two nonequivalent control group designs with the findings from a classical experimental design. Before-after designs without control groups overestimated program effectiveness and the nonequivalent control group designs underestimated program effectiveness [17].

Example 5.   To assess the effectiveness of small-group meetings in improving the level of knowledge about, and receptivity to family planning practices, a group of researchers in Taiwan conducted interviews with a random sample of women in the target villages. About six months after the meetings had been held, the sample was again interviewed. Those who had attended the meeting became the experimental group and their responses were compared with those who did not attend the meeting (the nonequivalent control group) [18].

Combination Time Series and Nonequivalent Control Group Design. Adding a control group to the conventional time series design provides a much more rigorous design than the conventional time series design or the nonequivalent control group design. The combination is diagrammed as follows.

	Before Measurements	Exposure to Program	After Measurements
Experimental group	$O_1 O_2 O_3 O_4$	X	$O_5 O_6 O_7 O_8$
Control group	$O_A O_B O_C O_D$		$O_E O_F O_G O_H$

Note that the nonequivalent control group design is contained within this design $\begin{pmatrix} O_4 & X & O_5 \\ O_D & & O_E \end{pmatrix}$, but the combination design rules out all threats to internal validity. The multiple measurements before program exposure will point out any differences existing between the two groups, so any effects of program exposure are more easily interpreted. The availability of relevant routinely-reported data places limits on the usefulness of this design, but these data exist in many organizations.

This design is one of the better quasi-experimental designs and is especially useful in assessing the impact of programs established in some subunits of an organization and not in similar others.

Example 6. In response to a perceived rapid increase in gang delinquent behavior, a community instituted an intensive intervention effort based on a "total community" effort. As a part of the evaluation of the effort, youths in the "target" groups were compared with control groups (youths not contacted as part of the intervention program). Among the measures used were the number of court appearances per year over time and the number of individuals appearing in court per year over time [19].

COMPARATIVE DESIGNS. *Comparative design* is a rubric used to classify a wide variety of evaluation approaches. It is not so easily diagrammed in the same way as experimental designs. Whether comparative designs are quasi-experimental or nonexperimental is a topic for debate, but the basic process of all evaluation is *comparison* regardless of the design. Experiments compare outcomes in two groups, equated by randomization, only one of which has been exposed to the experimental variable. Comparative designs are simply those study designs that compare the relative merits, advantages, or effectiveness of two or more programs, subprograms, or program elements without benefit of randomization and experimental isolation. These designs represent attempts to isolate the impact of programs, subprograms, or program elements on outcomes by identifying and comparing similarities and differences among programs with similar objectives. Proponents of comparative designs find them useful in assessing relative advantages of different programs with similar objectives, in determining the relative effectiveness of program elements within single programs, in building standards in areas where explicit standards do not exist, and in generally assisting program improvement.

Ideally, the logic of comparative designs is straightforward. If two or more programs are similar in all aspects but one and differ in effectiveness, it is plausible to assume that the one aspect on which they differ accounts for the difference in effectiveness. For example, if a large number of mental health programs that rely on chemotherapy are more effective in reducing length of hospitalization, the investigator is likely to conclude that chemotherapy reduces the length of hospital stay. If this finding holds across numerous programs that are identical in all other important aspects, impressive evidence points to the effectiveness of chemotherapy in reducing length of stay in mental hospitals. In this instance other program elements and aspects are ruled out as possible factors in reducing length of hospitalization in the sense that these were common to all programs and variations in ongoing programs that, theoretically, could provide alternative explanations for the dependent variable were also absent.

Comparative designs are useful in building standards of effectiveness in programs for which unambiguous standards are rare. For example, few ongoing programs have explicit quantified objectives, and even in those cases in which objectives are explicit and quantifiable, programs almost always vary in the extent to which they achieve a portion of their objectives over a given time period. The question of effectiveness thus becomes empty unless there are standards of performance. That is what portion or percentage of objectives are *expected* to be attained during a set time period?

For example, a public mental hospital may have seven

geographic units, all of which have the same objectives. Although not often the case, suppose these objectives are quantified such that the effectiveness of each geographic unit is easily determined, and a study reveals that the units ranged from 40 to 80 percent on a continuum of effectiveness with a range of 0 to 100. Lacking an overall standard, several conclusions are possible. The most apparent conclusion is that all units achieved less than 100 percent; therefore, all units are ineffective. Or, the objectives were unrealistic to begin with and all units were effective. A third is that the worst unit was 40 percent effective according to the criteria, the best unit 80 percent, and the others somewhere in between.

Unless some expected standard exists against which program effectiveness can be measured, effectiveness measures have little meaning. Effectiveness measures almost always depend upon the reasonableness of goals or objectives. Seldom are the expected standards of performance explicitly stated. In the above example all units could be highly effective if the expected levels of performance were the attainment of 20 percent of the objectives within the time covered by the study; conversely, all units could be ineffective if the expected level were 90 percent.

A comparative design could, of course, be used to develop an empirically based standard. The average effectiveness of the seven units becomes a standard against which to measure individual unit effectiveness. Similarities and differences in above-average and below-average units are then used to explain unit effectiveness. Or the average effectiveness of the seven geographic units could be indicative of the effectiveness of the geographic unit system as a whole. In this instance the variations in delivery of services that are unique to low and high effectiveness units tend to average out, and the overall effectiveness score is more representative of the geographic unit systems. In a large number of similar programs comparative designs shade into multivariate, correlational, and other statistical designs; but the logic remains the same.

Statistical techniques such as multivariate and covariance analyses *approximate* controls used in experimental designs [20].

Example 7. Comparative analyses clearly do qualify as quasi-experimental designs if a normative baseline against which program outcomes can be compared exists. To evaluate various mental health activities, James Ciarlo and associates [21] designed a number of scales reflecting social functioning and intrapersonal comfort. These scales were administered to samples of patients on admission and follow-up and were also administered to a random sample of persons in the community. These scores are used as a norm, and program success is defined as follow-up scores equal to or better than the first standard deviation below the mean of the normative sample. Because the normative sample is not "posttested," this design does not fit the previously discussed experimental model; yet it is a quasi-experimental comparative design.

Comparative designs provide an ideal means of ruling out many assumptions regarding relationships between program elements and program outcomes and of pointing out relevant relationships to be checked by more rigorous experimental designs. If evaluation efforts are directed toward providing alternative approaches, comparative designs can be used to suggest the best possible programs, subprograms, and program elements.

Although comparative designs have many advantages, they do not present a panacea for evaluation. The major problems of applying these designs are associated with the problems of measurement and program change. Few programs are designed with precise variations among them for the evaluator to use in analyzing the similarities and differences so necessary for comparative designs. Because of the state of theoretical knowledge about the processes of service programs, separating relevant differences between programs and measuring their impact on program effectiveness are difficult. Because many service programs have only small effects on a target population and programs contain numerous uncontrolled variations, the task becomes cumbersome and exploratory, requiring a great deal of statistical expertise, time, and money. Few programs have the resources necessary for such evaluations.

Although the problem is not unique to comparative designs, programs tend to shift and change as a result of trying one approach, discarding it, and trying another. Program change almost always creates havoc for evaluators. When program change occurs during the data-gathering stage, comparisons become meaningless; when it occurs any time afterward, comparisons become anachronistic. It is almost impossible to maintain such control over program operation that variables used in a comparative evaluation remain relatively unchanged. Changing goals, objectives, program structures, processes, resources, and a variety of other factors make long-term comparative studies impractical; but if the present emphasis on the development of program standards, management information systems, and other routine program monitoring systems continues, data will become more readily available to evaluators, thus making comparative designs more useful.

BARGAIN BASEMENT DESIGNS [22].   The world in which program evaluation takes place is complex and messy. Drastic change often occurs during the evaluation because programs change during their course of operation. Objectives may be changed, new personnel and techniques introduced, budgets increased or decreased, services added or deleted, or the target population altered. Expensive evaluations of a single program may be useless if the program no longer exists in the same form. Most often anything approaching experimental isolation is not possible or practical. Neat rigorous experimental designs that have been productive in other areas are difficult to apply and are rarely used in program evaluation. The logic and utility of multiprogram comparative designs are not widely accepted by program administrators, and these designs may be considered too costly and time consuming.

Because bad evaluation can be worse than no evaluation at all, the question arises: When designs with high internal validity are not possible and comparative designs are inappropriate, what designs are available for the job? The answer, of course, depends on the type of evaluation question and whether program standards exist. But in many instances simple designs may be appropriate. For example, the purpose of an evaluation study may be to explicate structures or processes of programs to gain insight into program operations. The question is: What is really going on? Explicit program standards are sometimes available, and the purpose of evaluation may be to determine if a program meets these standards. The question here is: How does a program compare with existing standards? Hospital accreditation and quality control activities fall into this category, and as noted in the definitions, are considered evaluation activities under certain circumstances. For these purposes, when designs with high internal and external validity are not necessary, bargain basement designs can provide the necessary information.

Many evaluations use bargain basement designs because they provide a way to answer many of the questions posed by administrators, and they are relatively cheap, simple, and quick. Of the 31 evaluation designs reported in studies published in the *American Journal of Public Health* and *HSMHA Health Reports* in 1970 and 1971, 14 (45 percent) were bargain basement (single-group before-after) designs. However, a review of 356 evaluations in the field of mental health showed that 40 percent of them did have controls of some sort [14]. Skillfully and conscientiously done, bargain basement designs can produce interesting qualitative information about program structures and processes and the extent to which standards are met. They also point to problem areas deserving additional exploration. Studies with bargain basement designs can guide investigators through a complex maze of program structures and processes and can suggest workable solutions for many problems faced by program administrators. These designs can also suggest policy and program inadequacies, although they lack the precision of scientific analysis. All too often, however, these designs are used inappropriately to indicate program impact or program effectiveness, a use that is possible only with certain types of information.

The simplest (and weakest) of these designs is the one-program after-only design, diagrammed as (X O_1). Having no preprogram measures and no control group, the evaluation describes the current status of the program or of clients. There is no basis for comparison in the design, and regardless of how well data are manipulated, the design yields only unsupported assumptions about the influence of X on O_1. Several popular variations of this design include attempts to establish some "standard" against which to compare findings. For example, relevant data on clients may be available from records, or the investigator may ask former participants retrospectively to relate their attitudes, feelings, or conditions prior to participating in the program. Retrospective self-reports tend to be biased by the present state of affairs, and records may often be inadequate so that no basis for comparison can be generated. Occasionally, however, programs may have set goals and defined criteria of success in such a way that an after-only design, although still weak, is nevertheless adequate for the program manager. Goals such as "no rehospitalization," "abstains from alcohol," "gainfully employed," "no record of arrest," and so on are goals and criteria that require only postprogram measurement. This may be quite sufficient for the manager, despite the fact that the contribution of the program to the outcome cannot be determined.

The extent to which a target population has changed from some pre- to postcondition can be measured in a relatively inexpensive way with the one-program before-and-after design (O_1 X O_2). This design usually is based on the assumption that the $O_1 - O_2$ difference is brought about by the program (X). However, because random assignment and control groups are not part of the design, effects of the program are difficult to separate from other events that occurred between pre- and post-measures. This design is more appropriately used in situations in which nonprogram factors can be ruled out as influences on the evaluation criteria O_1 and O_2. An interesting application of this design is a comparison of planned results with actual results. Program accomplishments in many programs are planned a year or so in advance, usually without knowing a program's effectiveness. This design allows a relatively simple inexpensive assessment of how well planned results were accomplished. O_1 would be the specified goals or objectives of the program, X the program activities over a set time period and O_2 the actual performance of the program in meeting specified goals or objectives. [22:62–63] This design is often incorporated into planning.

Another popular bargain basement design is the two-group, after-only design $\begin{pmatrix} X & O_1 \\ & O_2 \end{pmatrix}$. The design assumes the two groups were similar before one group participated in the program and that any difference between O_1 and O_2 is the result of program exposure. Here again, the lack of random assignment negates unambiguous assessment of program influences, but careful selection of a comparison group so that both groups are similar in all important criteria except program exposure increases the credibility of this design. This design is especially useful if the comparison group is made up of persons who will at some later time be exposed to the program and if measures are taken over several time periods. A relatively weak bargain basement design thus becomes a quasi-experimental design.

$$\begin{pmatrix} X & O_1 & & & \\ & O_2 & X & O_3 & \\ & & & O_4 & X & O_5 \end{pmatrix}$$

An appropriate evaluation design fits the specific problem addressed, controls for alternative explanations of the findings, and logically demonstrates relevant answers to the questions posed. Along with selecting the design, a concomitant task consists of selecting relevant evaluation criteria and mechanisms for obtaining necessary data.

EVALUATION CRITERIA. All researchers face general problems of finding and developing appropriate criteria to reduce by some operational procedures that portion of reality under observation so that it can be analyzed by acceptable methods and techniques. In the more complex evaluative research studies, uncertainties center around whether the measures "capture" the essence of the phenomena under investigation and the reasonableness of the assumptions made in simplifying the object of investigation (see "validity").

Seemingly simple data such as the aims of a program, the expected impacts or benefits, operating strategies and techniques, and other factors associated with programs are difficult to isolate. Unambiguous standards that allow ready comparisons are rarely available, and the longitudinal studies of program impacts needed to develop reasonable short- and long-term standards and measures of effectiveness are usually beyond the resources of individual programs. Thus, developing program criteria that have broad consensus is probably the most difficult task associated with program evaluation. If standards exist or if measurable goals or objectives are established, selecting criteria for evaluation becomes less problematic, but even so, problems of measuring goal attainment in effectiveness studies remain.

There is some controversy concerning whether the process of evaluation includes formulating a set of measurable program objectives or whether this task is part of program planning. However, evaluation of program effectiveness is not possible unless intended impacts of the program are stated in clearly measurable terms.* A set of procedures called "the Delphi technique" is useful for building specific measurable objectives for evaluating a program that lacks them [24]. The Delphi technique is a relatively simple straightforward procedure designed to elicit reliable consensus from a group of program personnel. A group of knowledgeable program personnel are asked individually to generate a list of program objectives. These lists are edited and a revised set of objectives is returned to each participant, who reviews and adds or deletes objectives as needed. The process continues until consensus is reached on a comprehensive set of objectives. Each participant is asked to assign weights to each objective, and the average weights are calculated. This back-and-forth process continues until program personnel have reached consensus concerning the objectives and their relative importance (weights).

The same technique can be used to generate a list of indicators for program effectiveness. Starting with the objectives, participants are asked to list indicators that could be used to measure the extent to which a program has achieved these objectives; then the process described above is put into effect. Use of the Delphi technique requires close cooperation between evaluators, planners, and

---

* *Program objectives* and *program goals* are used interchangeably in this section to indicate the specific state of affairs intended to be brought about by the program. A program objective or goal is simply an intended impact on the program itself or on some target population. For an insightful discussion of goals, see Lawrence B. Mohr [23].

program personnel if the results are to be meaningful and not merely an academic exercise [25, 26].

Regardless of the technique used to establish or operationalize program objectives and indicators, objectives should refer to tangible changes in behavior status or performance agreed upon by evaluators and program personnel, and indicators should clearly be appropriate for measuring these objectives. Consensus decreases the use of arbitrary measures and judgments and increases the chances that the results of evaluation will be accepted by program personnel.

DATA SOURCES AND DATA-GATHERING TECHNIQUES

[27, 28]. Once the type of information needed is determined, the next concern is selecting sources of data and techniques for gathering them. Some possible data sources are:

1. Existing records and statistics, including other evaluation and research studies
2. Competent program personnel
3. Clients
4. Citizens-at-large
5. Knowledgeable individuals outside the program
6. Program activities

Techniques of gathering data include:

1. Observation (analysis of records, recording events, obtaining physical evidence)
2. Questionnaires
3. Surveys and interviews

4. Tests
5. Subjective ratings by professionals
6. Direct measurements, such as clinical examinations

A lot of information is routinely collected in almost all programs and, therefore, if relevant to the purposes of evaluation, represents a savings of time and money in the data-collection process.* These data may range from responses gathered from client-intake interviews to detailed statistics concerning program productivity, costs, and processes. The quality, validity, reliability, consistency, and completeness of available data, however, often leave much to be desired because record keeping traditionally has been a !ow priority task in most organizations. There is also apt to be considerable variability among records for similar programs, which reduces their usefulness for comparative evaluations.

In spite of these shortcomings, existing records and documents often provide the only available source of information for evaluation, especially for time series designs.

As a technique of gathering data, *observation* has the advantage that it is independent of the subject's ability and willingness to report and it permits recording of behavior that is not dependent upon retrospective accounts. However, this technique is very costly, requires considerable expertise, and may not be practical.

Questionnaires are relatively inexpensive, lend

---

* This proliferation of data sometimes poses problems of confidentiality for evaluation studies. Technical safeguards, such as coding to conceal individual names and aggregating individual data items, are necessary parts of evaluation planning. Mechanisms to protect individuals should be clearly specified and agreed upon by program personnel, administrators, and evaluators prior to actual data gathering.

themselves to statistical analysis and can gather data from a large sample simultaneously. The problem of poor returns limits the use of questionnaires. The nature of the target population (e.g., children, illiterates) may also make the use of questionnaires inadvisable.

Interviews, although more expensive than questionnaires, allow more extensive and more accurate data about attitudes, opinions, and reported changes in behavior to be gathered. Interviews also allow rephrasing of questions to increase the respondent's understanding of what is asked. However, the presence of the interviewer sometimes predisposes respondents to answer in certain ways.

Other techniques of gathering data, such as tests, ratings, direct measurements, may fit the needs of evaluation. As with data sources, data-gathering techniques are numerous, limited mostly by the demands of the situation and the ingenuity of the investigator [29–32].

VALIDITY AND RELIABILITY.   In some programs goals are stated in concrete terms, and evaluation consists of relatively direct assessments of goal attainment. For example, a goal of a community mental health center may be to increase consultation to schools by 10 percent during a given time period. In this instance, the criterion is the amount of consultation, and effectiveness evaluation consists of counting the number of consultations at the beginning and end of a given time period. Although there may be some difficulties in determining exactly what constitutes a consultation (e.g., face-to-face, by telephone, letter, referral), there is no question about whether we are measuring what we claim to measure.

Direct measures and criteria are not always available, and evaluation must rely on indirect assessments and inferences to measure the consequences of programs. For example, there may be no behavioral attributes of clients and staff that unambiguously point out the differences between custodial and therapeutic programs in mental health. There may be no yardsticks available to clearly determine the impact of a social program on a target population. If no direct measures are available, indirect techniques may have to be invented. Indirect measures necessitate consideration of the problems of validity and reliability. *Validity* refers to the question: Are we measuring what we claim to measure? *Reliability* refers to the consistency with which a measuring device yields identical results when measuring identical phenomena. In the discussion of designs, internal and external validity were used to indicate how well a design produced the desired result—that is, the soundness of a design in determining the effects of a program (internal) and the extent to which findings could be generalized to other programs (external). Here validity refers to how well a measure (e.g., test, scale) captures the essence of the phenomenon of interest. For more detailed discussion of these concepts, the reader should consult other texts [33–35].

Validity. Validity is a complex and controversial issue involving inquiries into the nature and meaning of the program to be evaluated. The matter of validity is often ignored although indirect measures are used and all inferences drawn are premised on accurate valid measures. Infrequent use probably results from the facts: The theory and measurement of validity developed primarily in educational psychology, interval levels of measurement are used, and many instruments developed in evaluation rely on less than interval level measurements.*

Although there are several kinds of validity, the three types most generally accepted are criterion, content, and construct [34, 37–40].

Criterion validity refers to the relationship between an indirect measure and a more direct measure of the concept (criterion). In other words, a measure has criterion validity to the extent that it produces the same result as a more accepted measure. If an accepted criterion exists, it is not difficult to devise another measure and to establish statistically the extent to which the devised measure predicts the same result as the criterion. Often, unfortunately, criteria do not exist or their acceptance is doubtful.

Content validity refers to the degree to which items in the measurement instrument are representative of the content of the particular concept under consideration. Content validity has no statistical measure but is based on expert judgments. The basic questions before the judges are: Is using this item to measure this concept reasonable? Do the items of this measure represent a reasonable sample of all items that could be included?

Construct validity refers to *why* an instrument succeeds in measuring what it is supposed to measure. The three types of construct validity are nomological, convergent, and discriminant. *Nomological validity* refers to the extent to which a measure of a concept correlates with measures of other concepts as predicted by some theory. *Convergent validity* refers to the correlation between measures of the

* The four levels of measurement are the nominal, ordinal, interval, and ratio scales [36].

same concept using maximally different methods. *Discriminant validity* is obtained when concepts that are expected to be different on theoretical grounds do not yield high correlations between their measures. Measuring construct validity requires a great deal of methodological and statistical expertise, but it provides powerful support for indirect measures.

Reliability. *Consistency, stability,* and *reliability* are synonymous and are necessary characteristics of interpretable measuring instruments. Reliability refers to consistencies in measurement as determined by observed scores or ratings. The less error made in measuring a concept, the greater the reliability [33].

Methods of estimating reliability involve comparing at least two applications of the same instrument or equivalent instruments and determining the extent to which they agree. The closer the agreement, the greater the reliability. The *test-retest* method administers the same instrument to the same sample on two different occasions. The *equivalent-forms* method uses two versions of an instrument given to the same sample of respondents. The *split-halves* method divides the same instrument into two parts. In each method a statistical measure is calculated to assess the extent to which the two administrations, versions, or halves agree.

Most researchers agree that validity and reliability are important, but exactly how valid or how reliable an indirect measuring instrument must be remains an open question.

EMERGING APPROACHES TO EVALUATION. Ideally, evaluation studies are done to provide rapid but valid information for a variety of purposes. Evaluations in which an attempt is made to present valid generalizable findings are, however, rare and the "quick and ready" study predominates. Given the present state of the art, evaluations in which the attempt is made to provide valid and reliable findings must rely on traditional research designs, models, and techniques to select, collect, organize, and analyze data. As indicated earlier, the difficulties involved in fitting these designs to ongoing programs are many; consequently, evaluations are often attempted without benefit of adequate frameworks or with inappropriate methodologies. But the problems inherent in combining scientific principles with administrative and management concerns do not disappear when designs and methodologies proven successful in research endeavors are applied to answer evaluation questions. For example, the shortcomings of experimental designs outside the laboratory include lack of adequate controls over program elements and program participants; and quasi-experimental and bargain basement designs often fail to isolate the effects of program participation from the effects of other factors, and the results are ambiguous.

The need for valid and reliable information that is timely and appropriate for program managers continues to present dilemmas for both evaluators and administrators. Defining as program evaluation those studies that provide timely and appropriate information and defining as evaluative research, program outcome research, and generalizable research those studies that are less timely and appropriate but closely follow the canons of scientific inquiry, at best, begs the question. Under this scheme, program evaluation studies determine the extent to which a program meets its goals or objectives, the problems being encountered, and the side effects being created. Evaluative research utilizes scientific research methods and techniques for the purpose of evaluating a program. Program outcome studies establish the impact of a program on some target population. Generalizable research produces scientific knowledge by applying scientific research principles to the testing of a theory [41].

Many frameworks have recently been developed that make goals, processes, and outcomes of individual program participants more explicit and make program effectiveness evaluation an integral part of program process. Developed by practitioners to fit a limited range of mental health and rehabilitation programs, several of these approaches are receiving wide attention and may be applicable to a variety of programs. These techniques are continuously being tried, refined, and tried again; therefore, we mention them only briefly here. An accurate, up-to-date description of each should be obtained prior to their application.

In these emerging evaluation schemes the individual is focussed on as the unit of analysis, which necessitates developing client files (case histories that contain information on preselected variables) aggregating information for analysis and providing information based on the behavior and attitudes of individuals in particular situations. These models do not necessarily provide generalizable findings, but they do produce information detailing the positive aspects of a specific program and those aspects in need of improvement. They have also been used to compare program elements, intervention modalities, and even different practitioners.

EMERGING GOAL ATTAINMENT MODELS. Four emerging approaches to program evaluation that use individual goal attainment models are receiving wide attention as models for evaluating human services programs.

Models	Developers
Concrete Goal Setting (CGS)	Theodor Bonstedt, M.D.
Goal Attainment Scaling (GAS)	Thomas J. Kiresuk, Ph.D.
Goal-oriented Automated Progress Note (GAP)	Richard H. Ellis, Ph.D. Nancy Wilson, R.N., M.A.
Patient Progress Record (PPR)	Gilbert Honigfeld, Ph.D. Donald F. Klein, M.D.

These four approaches differ from the goal attainment model in that they provide for goal setting as a regular program activity and facilitate assessment of goal-method-outcome relationships. These models focus on goals of individual clients and the extent to which they are attained. However, aggregated individual goal attainment measures can be used to evaluate programs. They provide timely feedback and can lead to rapid improvement in the delivery of services, thus meeting one of the requirements of program evaluation. Although all of these approaches are too new to allow an accurate assessment of their utility and impact as models for evaluation, they do represent rather ingenious, albeit simple, approaches to providing criteria for program evaluation activities. Detailed descriptions of the four models have been presented in several publications and we only briefly summarize them here [42, 43].

Concrete Goal Setting (CGS).   Essentially a record keeping system, CGS provides for systematic review of a client's progress. A record (5 × 8 card) is created for each client containing the date of review, concrete goals for the client, methods or techniques for aiding the client to reach goals, staff personnel with major responsibility for client, and date of next review. The data generated by this approach can be used for assessments of client goal attainment, comparisons of methods or techniques most effective in aiding clients to reach goals, and if aggregated across all clients of a program, provide a rough measure of program effectiveness.

Goal-oriented Automated Progress Note (GAP). The approach of GAP is slightly more elaborate than the CGS approach, but it is essentially a method to describe the client's problems, set realistic goals, and select appropriate methods for reaching the goal efficiently. Staff members select appropriate goals from a list of 703 goal statements grouped into five major categories: medical, symptom, self-concept, client-initiated interaction, and disposition plan. Attached to each goal statement are two scales—one indicating the importance of this goal for this client and the other for recording client movement toward or away from this goal. Methods to be used are also rated by the staff. Staff members (and others, if desired) make ratings on progress toward initial goals at specified intervals and also review goals and methods for adequacy. Evaluation consists of aggregating success scores and disseminating these to appropriate managers.

Goal Attainment Scaling (GAS). Perhaps the best known of the four goal attainment approaches, GAS measures a client's progress toward attainment of any number of goals.

After one or two interviews, program personnel and a client negotiate any number of goals to be attained by the client. Goals are assigned weights relative to other goals, and a client's level at the beginning of treatment is determined. Goal attainment levels are in gradients of expected outcomes.

a. Most unfavorable treatment outcome thought likely   (−2)
b. Less than expected success with treatment   (−1)
c. Expected level of treatment success   (0)
d. More than expected success with treatment   (1)
e. Best anticipated success with treatment   (2)

For example, assume one goal for a client concerns education, assigned a relative weight of 20.*

Scale 1: Education ($w_1 = 20$)

(−2)   Patient has made no attempt to enroll in high school.

(−1)   Patient has enrolled in high school but at time of follow-up has dropped out.

(0)   Patient has enrolled but misses more than a third of the classes during a week.

(1)   Patient has enrolled, is in school at follow-up and attends classes consistently but has no vocational goals.

(2)   Patient has enrolled, is in school at follow-up, attends classes consistently and has some vocational goal.

* Adapted from Thomas J. Kiresuk [42:15].

Levels at intake are subtracted from levels at completion of program, and the resulting score is a measure of client change. Change scores are aggregated, and with the use of a formula developed specifically for Goal Attainment Scaling, program performance can be scored against an expected level of accomplishment and also for other kinds of comparisons.

Patient Progress Record (PPR). As a clinical goal-monitoring system, PPR is similar to the GAS in that goals (target areas) are set for individual clients, it is different in that scale values vary from 1 to 7 (1 being the desired state of affairs, 7 the more undesirable state). Goals are set for clients by the program staff and at specified time periods; each client's progress is reviewed by program personnel; and the client's level of goal attainment is ascertained. Initial goals and subsequent progress of individual clients are processed and stored by a computer, enhancing communications about the status of clients. Aggregation of findings can be used to estimate the effectiveness of various treatment programs.

MANAGEMENT SYSTEMS. There are a variety of popular management systems that are attempts to make goals, objectives, and other criterion measures more explicit and to gather information that will permit managers to make more effective decisions. Although not strictly evaluation models, a well designed management system can yield relative measures of cost and effectiveness for competing programs, allowing evaluation of a program's merits and more appro-

priate decisions concerning allocation of resources. Among
the currently popular management systems are Management by Objectives (MBO) [44–45] and Planning, Programming, and Budgeting System (PPBS).* Each requires
considerable time and commitment of resources to design,
operationalize, and maintain, but all of these management
systems, once implemented, provide more consistent and
accurate data for decision making than is usually available.
A less well known method, Key Factor Analysis [43, 46], differs from the others in that it combines the systems and
goal attainment models and explicitly incorporates the requirements of evaluation.

OTHER MODELS. A model for evaluation that is an attempt to bridge the gap between experimental research
models and descriptive case studies of undigested data is
the Multi-Attribute Utilities (Values) Model [47]. Essentially,
it is an approach to program planning and decision making
that elicits a set of expected outcomes, each weighted by
decision makers concerned with the program. These subjective estimates of the value of each program dimension
can be verified (or corrected) by comparing them with objective data. Marcia Guttentag [48] describes an application
of the model in the Office of Child Development, HEW,
and concludes that this approach eliminates many of the
problems resulting from attempts to fit experimental research designs to evaluation studies. In an earlier article

* PPBS, one of the innovations in management systems during the 1960s
was originally designed for the Department of Defense and widely accepted throughout the Federal Government, but present interest is now
shifting to other systems.

[49] Guttentag presents additional models and techniques for evaluation that are not tied to experimental research designs.

Another evaluation model that has recently emerged provides for continuous monitoring of client outcomes and the indirect impact of the program on other human service organizations (see Example 7). Essentially, this model uses follow-up interviews of ex-clients to establish levels of program effectiveness, and the focus of evaluation is on any change in the level of effectiveness over set time periods. Continuous monitoring refers to a continuing effort to measure the occurrence of various changes in certain characteristics of a target population. It is a powerful model with all the advantages of time series designs. However, the potential of monitoring rests on the availability of indicators that accurately reflect impacts of a program. The lack of adequate social indicators and the demand for quantitative data that serve as valid and reliable measures of important social characteristics of a target population have resulted in a flurry of interest and activity in the development of social indicators. Given the multifaceted approach of many social programs, the small impact these have on a population, and the difficulties of ruling out other factors, much basic work remains to be done. At present we depend on very gross indicators of program impacts on the assumption that any measure is better than nothing at all. Some of these problems are discussed in the following chapter.

CONCLUDING REMARKS. From among the many approaches to evaluation, the preferred approach makes valid, reliable, and applicable information available to decision makers. Difficulties associated with experimental designs in the real nonlaboratory world of ongoing programs limit their usefulness for evaluation, except for social experiments and demonstration projects.* Quasi-experimental designs are somewhat weaker in isolating cause-and-effect relationships, compared with experimental designs; but they offer an acceptable logic and considerable utility for evaluation purposes. These designs are not used so often as they could and should be. Most evaluations rely on the bargain basement designs which are the simplest and weakest of available study designs. Difficulties in isolating cause-and-effect relationships with bargain basement designs are usually insurmountable; but these designs, if used appropriately, can provide information about program structures, processes, and the extent to which program criteria are met.

We mentioned several emerging and sometimes competing approaches to evaluation which differ from most research models in that they focus on individual clients and they change the program to facilitate data collection. Probably a continuous-monitoring approach (a modified time-series design) promises the most utility for evaluation, although problems of what to monitor are great.

By fitting designs, models, and techniques to ongoing programs, valid, reliable, and applicable information can be provided which reflects the needs of program managers and contributes to the body of knowledge about ongoing

---

* Major social experiments, such as OEO's three-year negative income tax experiment in New Jersey; income maintenance experiments in Indiana, Colorado, and Washington; experiments involving housing allowances for low income people, health insurance, health services; and others are under way to test these policies before full-scale implementation. Social experiments are possible in many more instances than they are used.

programs. The factors that intervene between the production of such information and its acceptance and use by program managers are explored in the next chapter.

REFERENCES

1. Samuel H. Stouffer, "Some Observations on Study Designs," *American Journal of Sociology,* LV, 355–361 (1950).

2. Amitai Etzioni, "Two Approaches to Organizational Analysis: A Critique and a Suggestion," *Administrative Science Quarterly,* V, 257–278 (September 1960).

3. *Academy of Management Journal,* XV, entire issue (December 1972).

4. Donald T. Campbell and Julian C. Stanley, *Experimental and Quasi-Experimental Designs for Research,* Rand McNally, Chicago, 1966.

5. B. Botein, "The Manhattan Bail Bond Experiment," *Texas Law Review,* XLIII, 319–331 (1965).

6. Norman Chervancy and Gary Dickson, *An Experimental Evaluation of Information Overload in a Production Environment,* University of Minnesota: Management Information Systems Research Center Working Paper Series, 1972.

7. Benjamin Pasamanick, Frank Scarpitti and Simon Dinitz, *Schizophrenics in the Community: An Experiment in the Prevention of Hospitalization,* Appleton-Century-Crofts, New York, 1967.

8. Simon Dinitz, "Policy Implication of an Experimental Study in the Home Care of Schizophrenia," *Sociological Focus,* I (Winter 1967).

9. Ann E. Davis, Simon Dinitz, and Benjamin Pasamanick, "The Prevention of Hospitalization in Schizophrenia: Five Years After an Experimental Program," *American Journal of Orthopsychiatry,* XLII (April 1972).

10. R. L. Solomon, "An Extension of Group Control Design," *Psychological Bulletin,* XLVI, 137–150 (1949).

11. R. A. Fisher, *The Design of Experiments,* Oliver & Boyd, Edinburgh, 1935.

12. Susan Salasin, "Experimentation Revisited: A Conversation with Donald T. Campbell," *Evaluation,* I, 7–13 (#3, 1973).

13. Julian Stanley, "Controlled Field Experiments as a Model for Evaluation," in Peter Rossi and Walter Williams (eds.), *Evaluating Social Programs,* Seminar Press, New York, 1972, pp. 67–71.

14. Robert Hetherington et al., "The Nature of Program Evaluation in Mental Health," *Evaluation,* II, 78–82 (#1, 1974).

15. Donald T. Campbell, "Reforms as Experiments," *American Psychologist,* XXIV, 409–429 (1969).

16. B. G. Greenberg, "Evaluation of Social Programs," *Review of the International Statistical Institute,* XXXVI, 260–277 (#3, 1968). Reprinted in Francis Caro (ed.), *Readings in Evaluation Research,* Russell Sage Foundation, New York, 1971, pp. 155–175.

17. O. L. Deniston and I. M. Rosenstock, *Health Services Reports,* LXXXVIII, 153–164 (February 1973).

18. Laura Pan Lu, H. C. Chen, and L. P. Chow, "An Experimental Study of the Effect of Group Meetings on the Acceptance of Family Planning in Taiwan," *The Journal of Social Issues,* XXIII, 171–177 (October 1967). Reprinted in Francis Caro (ed.), *Readings in Evaluation Research,* Russell Sage Foundation, New York, 1971, pp. 391–396.

19. Walter B. Miller, "The Impact of a 'Total Community' Delinquency Control Project," *Social Problems,* X, 168–191 (#2, 1962). Reprinted in Frances Caro (ed.), *Readings in Evaluation Research,* Russell Sage Foundation, New York, 1971.

20. Hubert M. Blalock, Jr., *Social Statistics,* McGraw Hill, New York, 1960.

21. James Ciarlo and Jacquiline Reihman, "The Denver Community Mental Health Questionnaire: Development of a Multi-Dimensional Program Evaluation Instrument, mimeographed, 1975.

22. Harry P. Hatry, R. E. Winnie, and D. M. Fish, *Practical Program Evaluation for State and Local Government Officials,* The Urban Institute, Washington, D.C., 1973.

23. Lawrence B. Mohr, "The Concept of Organizational Goal," *The American Political Science Review,* LXVII, 470–471 (June 1973).

24. Norman Dalkey, *Delphi,* P-3704, Santa Monica, California: Rand Corporation, October 1967.

25. T. Mahoney, A. Annoni, and G. Milkovitch, "The Use of the Delphi Technique in Manpower Forecasting," *Management Science,* XIX (December 1972).

26. M. Skutsch and J. Schofer, "Goal Delphis for Urban Planning and Concepts in Their Design," *Socio-Economic Planning Science,* VII, 305–313 (1973).

27. Claire Selltiz et al. (eds.), *Research Methods in Social Relations,* Holt, Rinehart & Winston, New York, 1967.

28. Gideon Sjoberg and Roger Nett, *A Methodology for Social Research,* Harper & Row, New York, 1968.

29. E. J. Webb et al., *Unobtrusive Measures: Non-reactive Research in the Social Sciences,* Rand McNally, Chicago, 1966.

30. R. L. Gordon, *Interviewing Strategy, Techniques and Tactics,* Dorsey, Homewood, Ill., 1969.

31. A. N. Oppenheim, *Questionnaire Design and Attitude Measurement,* Basic Books, New York, 1966.

32. John Madge, *The Tools of Social Science,* Doubleday, Garden City, N.Y., 1965.

33. Fred N. Kerlinger, *Foundations of Behavioral Research,* Holt, Rinehart & Winston, New York, 1964.

34. J. Guilford, *Psychometric Methods,* 2nd ed., McGraw-Hill, New York, 1954.

35. E. Lindquist (ed.), *Educational Measurement,* American Council on Education, Washington, D.C., 1951.

36. S. S. Stevens, "On the Theory of Scales of Measurement," *Science,* 684, 677–680 (June 7, 1946).

37. American Psychological Association, *Standards for Educational and Psychological Tests and Manuals,* Washington, D.C., 1966.

38. L. Cronback, "Coefficient Alpha and the Internal Structure of Tests," *Psychometrika,* XVI, 297–334 (1951).

39. L. Cronback and P. Mechl, "Construct Validity of Psychological Tests," *Psychological Bulletin,* LII, 281–302 (1955).

40. L. Cronback, *Essentials of Psychological Testing,* 2nd ed., Harper & Row, New York, 1960.

41. Southern Regional Education Board, *Definition of Terms in Mental Health, Alcohol Abuse, Drug Abuse, and Mental Retardation,* National Institute of Mental Health Methodology Reports, #8, 1973.

42. "Four Ways to Goal Attainment, *Evaluation,* Special Monograph #1, 1973.

43. H. R. Davis, *Planning for Creative Change in Mental Health Services* (HSM 71-9057), Washington, D.C., National Institute of Mental Health. no date.

44. Douglas McGregor, "An Uneasy Look at Performance Appraisal," *Harvard Business Review* XXXV (May/June 1957).

45. Peter Drucker, *Practice of Management,* Harpers, New York, 1954.

46. Philip Longhurst, "Key Factor Analysis: A General Systems Approach to Program Evaluation," *Systems Approach to Program Evaluation in Mental Health,* Boulder, Colo. Western Interstate Commission for Higher Education, 1970, pp. 23–46.

47. Ward Edwards, "Social Utilities," *The Engineering Economist,* Summer Symposium Series, VI, 1971.

48. Marcia Guttentag, "Subjectivity and Its Uses in Evaluation Research," *Evaluation,* I, 60–65 (#2, 1973).

49. Marcia Guttentag, "Models and Methods in Evaluation Research," *Journal for the Theory of Social Behavior,* I, 75–95 (#1, 1971).

4

Problems and Pitfalls

Evaluators, evaluation sections, and evaluation centers have emerged in universities; local, state, and federal governments; and in public and private organizations. A myriad of evaluators produce hundreds of evaluations, many of which are methodologically sound and could be used for program innovation and program improvement. Yet the impact of evaluation findings on program innovation has been far less than expected. Even in those cases in which evaluators produce elegant and rigorous studies, few of the results are assimilated into decisions concerning program modifications. Much of the information supplied by evaluations is simply not used by program administrators and practitioners. When one considers the millions of dollars invested in evaluation and the sporadic and inconsistent utilization of evaluation results, the methodological issues discussed in Chapter 3 pale by comparison. As part of a growing literature addressed to this problem, Weiss reviewed evaluation activities that were described in 10 studies funded by NIMH or other federal agencies and concluded that underutilization of findings results more from organizational constraints on evaluators' activities than on the lack of methodological expertise [1].

Ideally, successful evaluation depends on the evaluator's ability to collect, organize, and relate data to meaningful patterns; to translate these patterns into a common conceptual framework shared with administrators and practitioners; and to feed the results back to administrators and practitioners in a manner most likely to be accepted. Equally important to the process of evaluation is the practitioner's willingness and ability to accept the results of evaluation, to integrate these results with other knowledge, and to create or modify, as justified, any or all aspects of program structure and process. Successful evaluation involves an interaction of methodology, bureaucracy, and politics. Suchman notes: "It is not so much the principles of research that make evaluation studies difficult, but rather the practical problems of adhering to these principles in the face of administrative considerations" [2:21].

Despite advances in methodology that make evaluation findings more applicable, decisions concerning programs are only partially related to variables such as costs, benefits, effectiveness, and impacts. Many problems associated with evaluation stem from an academic discipline-oriented focus and an attempt to apply research models to evaluation problems. But the problems of achieving an acceptable balance between providing information that is valid from a methodological point of view yet applicable from the practitioner's perspective will not cease to exist simply with a change in the focus of evaluation. A large variety of factors, ranging from a poor understanding of the purposes of evaluation to the pull of vested interests, influence the willingness and ability of evaluators and managers to realize the ideal situation. In this chapter we discuss some of these factors and constraints and mention various ways of "doing" evaluation in concert with the demands of practitioners and the constraints of organizational structures and processes [3].

THE PROCESS OF EVALUATION.   Evaluation consists of four phases: selection, execution, communication of the results, and implementation of the findings. The problems and pitfalls that emerge in each phase of the process are closely tied to the process itself.

Selecting a Program for Evaluation.   A program may be selected for evaluation because:

1. It is not operating according to expectations, and evaluation is considered necessary to formulate remedial action.
2. It requires evaluation to determine need for improvement or modification.
3. It is very successful and requires evaluation to determine whether elements responsible for success can be used elsewhere in the system.
4. It includes new technologies, and evaluation is necessary to determine their contribution to the program.

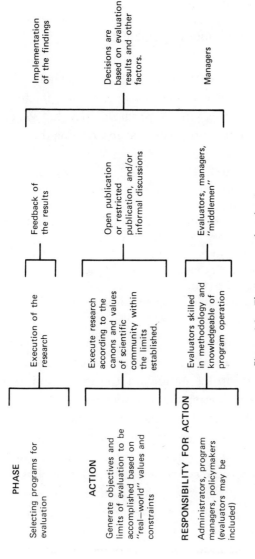

PHASE

Selecting programs for evaluation

Execution of the research

Feedback of the results

Implementation of the findings

ACTION

Generate objectives and limits of evaluation to be accomplished based on "real-world" values and constraints

Execute research according to the canons and values of scientific community within the limits established.

Open publication or restricted publication, and/or informal discussions

Decisions are based on evaluation results and other factors.

RESPONSIBILITY FOR ACTION

Administrators, program managers, policymakers (evaluators may be included)

Evaluators skilled in methodology and knowledgeable of program operation

Evaluators, managers, "middlemen"

Managers

Figure 4.1. The process of evaluation.

93

5. Evaluation is a well established part of program operation, and evaluations are routinely done.
6. Federal, state, or local agencies (usually those funding the program) require program evaluation.

The above are instances of program evaluation for bona fide purposes of learning about program effectiveness to improve the program. A program may be selected for evaluation for inappropriate reasons. Among these are:

1. Administrators are dissatisfied with program managers, and evaluation is to provide an "objective" basis for redistributing power.
2. The program is being challenged, and favorable evaluation is necessary to counter the attack.
3. Additional funds are needed to expand the program, and a favorable evaluation would increase the chances of obtaining these funds.
4. Funds are available for evaluation.

Most evaluations of social programs probably occur because funding agencies (usually the federal government) require some sort of evaluation for initial and continued funding. Some programs are evaluated simply because administrators want favorable state-of-the-program evaluations to convince a constituency of the program's merits. But an increasing number of programs are evaluated because managers are concerned with program effectiveness.

At this stage of the evaluation process—selecting a program for evaluation—many problems and pitfalls can be avoided by carefully previewing the methodological and political problems involved. The objectives and limits of the evaluation must first be based on "real world" values and constraints. For whom, by whom, and for what purpose is the evaluation to be conducted? What are the responsibilities of program administrators, managers, policymakers, practitioners, and evaluators? Who initiates the request for evaluation? Who controls the funds for evaluation activities? Is the evaluation to serve the program? Is it to judge the program's merits? How are the results of evaluation to be transmitted back to the program? Are the results to be openly published or are there restrictions? Is the political climate of the organization such that quality evaluation can be done? What happens if the evaluation produces favorable results? Unfavorable results?

These questions should be asked by evaluators, answered by administrators, and assuming both agree on their ability to carry out the particular evaluation project, this information provides the basis for assessing the extent to which the program *can* be evaluated. That is, if the evaluator is free to choose whether to evaluate the program selected by administrators and if he is satisfied with the conditions specified by administrators, he must then determine if there are sufficient resources (both expertise and money) committed to the project to permit successful evaluation under the accepted conditions. If the evaluator is located within the same system as the program, he often does not have such a choice. The evaluator in such a position could, of course, influence the selection of programs to be evaluated in much the same manner as administrators and for similar reasons. That is, he may enter into the political processes and attempt to manipulate decisions by using "real world" values and political processes (see Chapter 5).

What are the problems associated with the process of program evaluation described above?

For Whom?   Many of the problems encountered in evaluation arise out of unrecognized differences in the orientations of evaluators and program practitioners. By the nature
of their roles, practitioners tend to be advocates for their
programs, perhaps not so much because the program is
spectacularly successful but simply because they feel it is
better than nothing at all. Practitioners claim knowledge of
the program and its problems, and seldom do they expect
information from evaluations to be adequate for their purposes. In programs that depend partially or totally on
federal, state, local, and to a lesser extent, private funds,
practitioners see their already substantial reporting requirements as justifying their reluctance to invest any additional
resources in evaluation activities. Such investments, they
feel, detract from their capability of providing direct
services to clients, and further, evaluation offers no immediate payoff.

Practitioners are managing their programs in a political
world of negotiation and compromise. Their programs are
enmeshed in a matrix of values, assumptions, and objectives
that may or may not stress achieving program goals. Decision processes concerning program initiation, continuance,
and change do not necessarily place a lot of importance on
successful attainment of program goals nor on any of the
other variables so valued by evaluators. For the most part,
managers of social programs have little or no training in
program administration and management. Most frequently,
they are political appointees or clinicians who are
promoted to managerial positions because of seniority or
superior clinical skills. Their interests may center on attain-
ing more power, maintaining the status quo, or continuing
their clinical pursuits [4]. The politics of program survival
and the matrix of political relationships within which a

program operates are very real and important to *successful* program managers, but have been often ignored by evaluators and less successful managers. Evaluation is a special form of political interaction, more problematic than the usual because there is little consensus concerning the roles of program manager and evaluator.

Although the roles and orientations of evaluators are continuously changing toward producing more relevant evaluations, all too often evaluation is considered a means to a publication or a way to increase status in a discipline-related peer group. Evaluators who seek recognition from their discipline tend to perceive themselves as "objective" critics without vested interests in program outcome. Their interest in any program is temporary and particularistic. Their orientation and concern are directed toward producing valid and precise information that is suitable for publication in acceptable media.

The notion that reasonable approximations of ideal models are appropriate because they offer more useful, though less elegant, information and that *providing applicable information to program managers is what evaluation is all about* has not yet caught on. Great emphasis is placed on elegant quantitative models, and little attention is given to qualitative insights. Evaluators who are able methodologists tend to dichotomize evaluation into the categories of science and art. Methodologically sound studies filled with quantitative data fit the former; analyses that conform to models that are more understandable and acceptable to managers fit the latter. If the present trend toward relevancy continues, a third category that combines the pragmatism of management with the rigors of scientific investigation should emerge, albeit slowly.

An evaluation process that points in this direction is suggested by Gifford [15], who discusses the following stages:

1. Practitioners have a problem.
2. Evaluators work with practitioners to set objectives and measures of performance.
3. Evaluators gather preliminary data and create models relating resources to goals, goals to impacts, and impacts to benefits.
4. Evaluators, practitioners, and other interested parties discuss and suggest improvements of the models.
5. If models are not acceptable to all concerned, problems may be redefined, objectives restated, or appropriate alternative approaches detailed.
6. This process of iteration between evaluators and practitioners continues until problems, objectives, and methods of procedure are agreed upon prior to the research phase.
7. Evaluators perform evaluation and provide results to practitioners.

Gifford notes that this process is most effective when practitioners are supportive and interested in the outcome. Support and interest tend to occur when practitioners are convinced that the evaluation is relevant, timely, and possible, given the existing organizational constraints.

Evaluation is—or should be—focused on making recommendations for the improvement of program effectiveness as indicated by valid reliable information *and* in light of the existing political matrix within which the program operates. By using inputs from both practitioners and evaluators, those involved combine pragmatism and rigor and thereby make evaluation more relevant and increase the probability that recommendations will have impact on the program.

The above process may work simply because it combines the qualitative insights of practitioners with the quantitative data gathered by evaluators. In essence, this process provides for scientific investigation of essentially subjective problems, but its success depends heavily on the willingness of practitioners to make the initial move. The likelihood of this happening may increase because practitioners are participating more in defining the problems and approaches of evaluation, and they are thus more likely to initiate additional evaluations. Zusman and Ross [6], however, suggest that evaluators make the first move by choosing a model and then consulting with practitioners and clients of the program. But they emphasize that unless evaluators and practitioners agree on the methods and models to be used, the evaluation study is doomed either to fail or be disregarded by decision makers.

Responsibility for Evaluation.   Whose responsibility is it to decide whether a particular program will be evaluated? In the past evaluation activities have been imposed on program managers as a necessary but troublesome part of receiving federal funds for public programs. In some cases the requirements for evaluation consist of filling out long tedious forms and supplying data on program activities to agencies outside the program matrix [7]. In other cases annual evaluations are required, but they are usually isolated from program activities and have no impact on program operation. Wholey and White, in discussing the impact of program evaluation on Elementary and Secondary Education Act, Title I programs, an act that has very specific and comprehensive evaluation requirements, conclude: "the main purpose for evaluation, i.e., to feed back information about how a program is working to improve its operation is missing from most local and state evaluation activities" [8].

Evaluation is clearly the responsibility of management; but managers are often not fully aware of the role evaluation can play in decisions about programs, nor are they likely to gain this knowledge spontaneously. Understandably, when asked to justify their programs in terms of costs and impacts on clients or to design programs to remedy certain problems, administrators and managers seldom expect help from formal evaluations; nor can evaluators point to many clear instances in which evaluations have contributed to programmatic decisions. Somewhat more optimistically, the emerging models for evaluation, discussed in Chapter 3, tend to make evaluation an integral part of ongoing programs. In addition, evaluation is in vogue; and practitioners who are supposed to be adroit in evaluation, management consultants, and others concerned with administration and management are producing numerous articles calling for increased evaluation activities and elaborating on the utility of evaluation for decision making.* The effects of this trend could be profound. Evaluation may become *accepted* as an integral part of program management. Resources presently used for one-shot evaluations via contracts with outside agencies could then be shifted to in-house evaluation activities and the cost/benefit ratio of evaluation information would decrease [9]. Clearly this would place responsibility for specification of the evaluation problem squarely with management, but it could also raise some basic questions concerning the division of responsibility for the *execution* of evaluations. As

---

* See, for example, issues of *Community Mental Health Journal, Educational Technology, Management Controls, Management Accounting, Training and Development Journal, The Journal of Management Studies, Personnel Journal,* and many organizational journals.

noted by Caro [10], discipline-oriented evaluators claim ultimate responsibility for evaluation design and execution even though they have not been able to exercise sufficient control over program activities to fulfill this responsibility.

For What Purposes?   Programs may be selected for evaluations for many reasons (some are listed earlier in this chapter). However, evaluations have been classified into two broad categories—formative and summative—based on the types of information provided and how the information is used [11]. Formative evaluation provides information to improve programs during their developmental stages. Summative evaluations provide information for judging the worth or merit of a developed program.

These distinctions, developed primarily to apply to evaluation of an educational curriculum, are not so easily made in evaluations of ongoing social programs. First, social programs seldom emerge completely processed entities; rather, they continuously change or develop. In addition, rarely are unfavorable judgments of worth or merit made without an attempt to improve the program [12:7]. Using the formative-summative classification, one can classify evaluations as formative, summative-formative, or summative. Most evaluations of social programs would then fall into the summative-formative category. That is, the worth or merits of a program are determined and, if unfavorable, information is provided for improvement.

Autonomy.   The organizational loci of evaluation units are discussed in Chapter 5 with advantages and disadvantages associated with the location—inside or outside—of evaluators vis-a-vis the organization containing the program to be evaluated. Here a more fundamental aspect of the evaluator's role—independence—is considered. Ideally, the evaluator's role is one of an objective observer, aware of but uncompromised by vested interests in the program being evaluated. Most people realize that if the evaluator is a subordinate staff member of the practitioners who manage the program, objective assessment of the program is difficult and credibility is questionable. The evaluator may identify with the program and thus be more likely to give it the benefit of any doubts. The evaluator is also likely to become too familiar with the ongoing program, accept its limitations as necessary accommodations to real world demands and, in doing so, fail to see these as items to be included in the evaluation. Not much is gained if evaluators see only problems and recommend only alternatives that are already known to program managers. Nor are evaluations performed by program personnel or evaluators controlled by program managers likely to produce valid assessments of a program's effectiveness, although such evaluations are likely to be more acceptable to program practitioners. Autonomy for the evaluator, which is necessary for quality evaluation and basic to the conduct of scientific inquiry, remains a subject for negotiation and has not yet been recognized as a particularly troublesome condition. The present trend toward making evaluation more relevant by increasing the joint participation of evaluators, managers, and, in some cases, users of service could decrease the autonomy of the evaluator and adversely influence the quality of the evaluation.

Scriven [11] argues that, from a pragmatic standpoint, lack of autonomy is not so important in formative evaluation as it is in summative evaluation. But, as indicated earlier, the distinction between formative and summative evaluation is often obscure in ongoing social programs. Joint participation by evaluators and managers might lead to less independence for evaluators in time schedules, specification of the objectives of the evaluation, and the selection of models used to gather and analyze data. It could even result in the surveillance of the evaluation process by program managers [13:38].

Morehouse points to the dangers of such rigid monitoring of evaluation activities: ". . . evaluators have had an incentive to oblige the agencies, serving to some extent as sophisticated apologists for program shortcomings, emphasizing positive accomplishments where possible and explaining (rationalizing) program weakness" [14:870].

The exact amount of autonomy necessary for the conduct of quality evaluation is not easily determined, but it is unreasonable to expect the standards of scientific inquiry to be met by evaluators who are unable to apply their expertise without being subject to attempts to influence results or to other forms of interference.

EXECUTION OF THE RESEARCH PHASE. However onerous the political nature of selecting programs for evaluation may be to the evaluator, it is likely to be more acceptable than attempts by program personnel to modify the rules of scientific inquiry. Miller, in describing an attempt to apply discipline-oriented research methodology to a real-world problem, points out some political aspects of the research phase:

> The client—or, as in our project, the monitoring agent—may offer suggestions and instructions as the research proceeds. These are usually accepted as persuasions to modify

or intensify work in a given direction. These come to the project director and are transmitted through his actions or instructions to the group researchers. Sometimes the reason is not understood, or it may be understood but resented as an outside idea, foreign to the group process, and emotionally rejected.

Scientific canons of rigor may be opposed by demands for exploratory or applied research on problems for which hypotheses and measurement tools cannot be readied. A researcher whose pride system has incorporated strict and rigid standards of craftsmanship may quail before problems whose solution requires simple exploration or vulgar practicality (especially if he does not see how he can get a published paper from it).

The requirements of expense accounts, security clearances, permission for entry to the research field, "logistic support," and numerous matters of red tape are often further irritations—a headache to researchers and director alike. [15:43]

* * *

The design reflects the twofold objectives: (1) to carry on basic research in morale (or personal adjustment) at the descriptive level, and (2) to work on personnel problems at the diagnostic level. The design thus reflects both the canons of basic research and the requirements of the client for operational results. The balance between these two foci was often beset by subtle pressures deriving from professional standards, on the one hand, and the practical concerns of the military officials, on the other. The research director who seeks to advance knowledge must see that the research work is so designed that the long-run concerns of basic science are carried along while, at the same time, good diagnostic studies of operational problems are produced that convince his client that research can be of service to him on the problems he faces *now*. He must persuade his staff of the importance of these twin demands, and he must protect them so that there is ample opportunity to achieve both basic and operational research. The basic research design of the Air Site Project grew out of these pressures, and it sought to satisfy them. [15:50]

Stressing the interaction between scientific canons and real-world values, Coleman [16] discusses several aspects of the real world (the world of action) in which the evaluator operates and compares these with the world of the discipline-oriented researcher. Coleman's discussion concerns policy research, but his observations are equally applicable to program evaluation. The quality of relationships between evaluators and managers and the adjudged adequacy of the evaluation appear to improve, and the threat that managers feel about evaluation tends to decrease as collaboration increases [17]. In the real world, programs operate on a *time* schedule with funding cycles, deadlines, activity stages, and such, whereas the world of discipline-oriented knowledge is timeless. *Jargon* of the world of action is different from the jargon of any academic discipline. Although both the real world and a discipline have *vested interests, control of resources, conflicts, reward systems,* and *norms,* these differ in that in the real world these factors can both initiate and be affected by the evaluation process.

Valid and Precise or Applicable? Usually, in discipline-oriented research, researchers define problems along theoretical lines, derive hypotheses for investigation, select and operationalize criteria, determine items that combine to predict these criteria, support or fail to support the hypotheses, generate additional hypotheses for future investigation and, if all goes well, publish the study for an audience that accepts (or at least comprehends) the methodology utilized. Problems encountered in this process may be major, but there are patterned ways, accepted by both researcher and audience, to deal with these problems. The researcher is concerned with producing a study in which acceptable procedures are used; the main concern is not the extent to which research findings apply to or work to change any real-world situation, present or future. Most often, discipline-oriented researchers make their assumptions explicit and rarely claim their research produces findings that are applicable without further research. This is pure research in pure culture.

The basic aim of evaluation is to produce applicable information, although many evaluators cling to a discipline-oriented approach. Demands are for immediate answers to questions concerning the impact of social programs on clients, an area in which there are practically no theories and few guidelines. Ideally, the evaluation problem is defined by practitioners; evaluators sharpen and operationalize criteria, as necessary, to transfer the problem from the world of action into a form appropriate for scientific inquiry. During this process evaluators and practitioners agree on the kind of information needed and the model for generating this knowledge. Evaluators gather and analyze data for the purposes of explaining to practitioners and managers the impact of the program, what strategy is used to manage it, if and why programs exist, and what can be done if the program does not meet expectations. The data may also be used for ancillary purposes such as rating, monitoring, and costing. Results are translated from the framework of scientific inquiry into the language of practitioners and managers to increase their understanding of the findings.

Evaluators must be sensitive to the political nature of evaluation and the political processes associated with program development and program operation. An evaluator must understand the practitioner's role, the extent to which the process and results of evaluation threaten the practitioner's perceived role, and the extent to which organizational constraints influence the practitioner's ability to respond to evaluation results in a positive manner.

A study conducted by discipline-oriented researchers must be valid and precise; the successful evaluator must produce a valid, precise, and applicable study. Some authors [11, 18] have noted that the particular uncompromising combination of circumstances, settings, and demands that characterize program evaluation serve to make it more difficult than any of its close relatives (e.g., discipline research, management, policy analysis). These authors suggest that, ideally, evaluators should have expertise in statistics, cost accounting, management, public relations, anthropology, sociology, political science, psychology, philosophy, and of course, the content of the program to be evaluated. Given this impossible set of qualifications, it is no surprise that there are few "fully qualified" evaluators, although there are hundreds so labeled and so employed.

The process of selecting and applying models, methodologies, and techniques to produce valid, precise, and applicable information *for practitioners and managers* is political because they must be acceptable to both evaluators and practitioners and, often, to policy makers. The tensions between validity and precision and applicability are often so great that the requirements of the former may have to be sacrificed in favor of the latter, at least in the short run. The dual role of scientific researcher (valid and precise) and intervener (applicable) is fraught with problems and is often difficult to maintain. As in the example from Miller's project, practitioners tend to exercise influence over the research phase of evaluation because their values prescribe that they are the ultimate judges of the validity of measurements; so evaluators, as researchers-interventionists striving to maintain the dual role relatively intact, must successfully deal with pressures from practitioners that would threaten the validity of the evaluation. Often they are not successful [19, 20].

Weiss [21] has suggested that the almost impossible task of maintaining dual roles can be avoided if two models are used—one based on the practitioner's values, assumptions, and goals and the other based on more theoretically relevant assumptions. The former would tend to satisfy demands for applicable information; the latter would improve the craft of evaluation. Even if such a division were operationally feasible, it could only decrease the intensity, not eliminate the inherent role contradiction. Nearly every suggested solution to the role contradiction also weakens the potential impact and credibility of the evaluation effort.

Evaluation, an interactional process between managers and evaluators, is characterized by a lack of clear-cut and consensual norms governing the interaction. Interactional problems are not unique to evaluation—exchanges between individuals are seldom without some difficulties. However, the particular nature of the interaction—the lack of consensus surrounding the roles of practitioner and evaluator, the misunderstandings about the purpose of evaluation, and the lack of a mutually acceptable payoff—makes the process of evaluation extremely difficult.

As an idealized process, evaluation involves utilization of the rules of scientific inquiry to provide accurate and relevant information for decision making. But the canons of scientific inquiry require theories, elegant and rigorous designs, precise measurements, and results couched in a cautious framework of tentativeness. The methodological problems of applying the canons of scientific inquiry to the study of complex real-world programs are enormous, but not insoluble. The crux of the problem is not simply lack of technologies to conduct evaluation *from the evaluator's perspective* (although this is surely part of the problem), but rather the failure of these technologies to produce information practitioners will use for decision making. All too often the conflict between valid and precise information and applicable information results in evaluation compromises that satisfy neither evaluators nor practitioners.

Not all agree that a scientific method or a set of rules for scientific inquiry exists:

> There is no scientific method as such . . . the scientist's procedure has been merely to do his utmost with his mind, no holds barred. . . . The so-called scientific method is merely a special case of the method of intelligence, and any apparent characteristics are to be explained by the nature of the subject matter rather than ascribed to the nature of the method itself. [22:144–145]

A scientific method, as the term is used here, contains a set of rules and procedures which allows the gathering of objective and precise data such that generalizations founded on one set of observations can be verified on all subsequent occasions, under like conditions, by any impartial observer using the same method [23].

Curtis G. Southard [24] suggests that of the three levels of evaluation, one (the third) is scientific. First-level evaluations are those in which an individual or group evaluates a program with criteria developed according to personal objectives and values. This is the kind of subjective evaluation that has characterized most of the history of social programs and, when found insufficient, was slowly replaced by more formal approaches. It remains the most frequent level of evaluation and in certain instances (those requiring judgments of ethics, intrapersonal change, satisfaction, and so on) the most appropriate. At the second level a group of experts evaluate the program on the basis of their knowledge of the program and similar programs. The prototype of second-level evaluation is the management consultant. It is considered in more detail in the following chapter. Clearly, the value of this approach is dependent solely on the value of the individual experts. At the third level, the measurement of the program's effectiveness follows acceptable standardized procedures, designs, and instruments of determined validity and reliability.

COMMUNICATION OF THE RESULTS.   "Either you give us reports we can't read or you discuss things we aren't really interested in." "Intelligent but naive." "Scholarly but ignorant." "Potentially valuable but not relevant for our program." "You don't really understand our problems." "Although interesting, you neglected to mention that our problems are caused by inadequate funding and a shortage of qualified personnel." These responses from practitioners succinctly describe evaluation results that failed to be assimilated by practitioners and managers and thus are not likely to impact on programs.

With equal cogency, but from an opposite perspective, evaluators argue that evaluation results are misinterpreted, distorted, ignored, or rejected. Practitioners do not read the results, or if they do, they don't understand the nature of scientific evidence and proof. Or practitioners simply reject findings that are not consistent with their notions of program success.

Many evaluation studies, regardless of cost or sophistication, are not accepted by practitioners and are therefore are not used [25]. Coleman [16] suggests that lack of acceptance is partly due to differing orientation and interests of practitioners and evaluators. The practitioner's criterion of interest is the usefulness of the results (for his purpose), whereas the evaluator's interest centers around the correctness of the results and the elegance of the presentation. Thus, personal values of practitioners, not scientific canons of objectivity and truth, govern the acceptance of recommendations provided by evaluations, regardless of the size, scope, and sophistication of the study.

Part of the acceptance problem may rest in the evaluator's unwillingness to view evaluation data as essentially political and evaluation results as only one of the many inputs in the decision-making process of practitioners. Campbell [26] notes that by understanding political realities and contributing to political processes, evaluators can educate administrators to the problems and possibilities of methodologically sound evaluations. Even under the most ideal circumstances, evaluation may fall into "information overload," and results may not be accepted by program practitioners. As Davis puts it:

> One problem may lie in the existence here of an old assumption: that sound information is awaited by eager users. That's rarely true unless the relevance of knowledge to solving one's problem is crystal clear. On the contrary, knowledge, particularly knowledge on effectiveness, can be a dread simply because it nearly always demands action—change in one's behavior. The only alternative options are to ignore it, belittle it, or sabotage its production. That isn't to condemn the people who spurn knowledge. The input of action-compelling knowledge is overloading many responsible people: it's small wonder that staff and administrators sometimes follow the lead of certain patients—failing to respond to overloading stimuli! [27:28]

Given the methodological problems of evaluation, their aura of scientific accuracy may cause practitioners to overvalue and overreact to evaluation findings [3]. Mushkin, noting that a number of national programs failed or are being reassessed because of critical evaluations, contends that "evaluation is being used as a decision-making tool more than it warrants, especially in light of the present state of scientific understanding and of the expectations placed upon evaluations by the public and its officials" [28]. The careful phrasing of evaluation results obtained by scientific methodology sometimes creates misunderstandings, and evaluators often do not translate their findings into language understandable to practitioners. In addition, the method of investigation and the nature of proof via objective investigation often require that the evaluator attempt to disprove rather than prove something.

Negative findings (findings that the program had no significant impact on a target population) are taken as evidence that the program failed. Given the complexity of many social programs, the fact that most were designed to have only a small impact on a target population, and the fact that most were established for essentially political rather than objective reasons, evaluation methodologies are inadequate to produce valid indicators of program success. But evaluations will probably have neither a positive nor negative impact on programs unless the results are relevant to the values and assumptions of decision makers. If evaluation results are quickly and readily accepted, as Mushkin suggests, they probably agree with the preconceptions of at least some decision makers who are in positions of power and who could influence or make decisions concerning program continuance.

The opposite danger is equally real. The fallibility of the methods available to program evaluation as well as the disparity between the magnitude of expected change and the change measured by instruments are frequently cited as reasons for dismissing evaluations. Suchman notes:

> A fairly common mistake in evaluative research is to confuse the failure of the program with that of the evaluation study. An evaluation study which fails to show any effect can be quite successful as an evaluation—it was the program which was unsuccessful. It is, of course, possible that the evaluation measures were not sensitive enough, or even incorrectly chosen, to show an effect, but, given a carefully conducted study, the burden of proof rests upon the program itself. [2:23]

There is, of course, no formula for the solution of the problems of acceptability and adequacy. The greatest possible degree of prior agreement as to the intents of evaluation, including specification of questions which cannot be answered, is perhaps the best guideline.

IMPLEMENTATION OF EVALUATION FINDINGS. Ultimately, decisions concerning social programs are political, not technical, and evaluation results that do not mesh with political strategies of decision makers are not likely to impact on programs. The implications of this fact cannot be ignored if evaluation is to be recognized as a legitimate aspect of ongoing programs and as a viable practice for skilled personnel. Despite considerable advances in research technology, there has been little progress in identifying and measuring specific factors of the political environment which may determine, in large part, the acceptance or rejection of any evaluation study. One notable exception was an attempt to design an evaluation system for the National Institute of Mental Health (NIMH) which was directly linked to their decision-making needs. The proposed system included "the development of several quantitative models which describe the interactions among program interventions, underlying assumptions, environmental factors, and decision-making processes" [29]. While noting that many of the recommendations have merit and some have been incorporated, NIMH did not implement all aspects of the recommended system. Although this was an attempt to make explicit the political aspects of program operation, the critique noted that the "heavily structured approach, as recommended, must be blended within the framework of a highly dynamic bureaucracy, and the informal arrangement of a real world which, at times, are far less structural in operation" [29].

Implementation of evaluation findings is a critical phase of the evaluation process. It is also one of the most troublesome in that rarely are the findings translated into meaningful action. Note that there are differences between implementing findings, considering the findings for implementation, implementing program change which are different from but related to the findings, and accepting the findings but taking no action. For example, assume the product of evaluation is methodologically sound information in support of program modification. It is also relevant, timely, and understandable; the changes recommended are well supported; and the changes fall within the manager's span of control. The issue is this:

Is evaluation successful if its recommendations for program change are:

1. Implemented in toto
2. Implemented in part
3. Considered for implementation but rejected
4. Not implemented, but other related program changes resulted from the evaluation
5. Not implemented, but other nonrelated program changes are made
6. Not implemented, no program changes are made
7. Not implemented and evaluation findings challenged

Most commentators would agree that evaluation is successful if its recommendations are implemented, either totally or in part, but many consider Items 3 through 7 as indicative of evaluation failures. Because implementation is the criterion of success for some evaluators, they consider implementation a necessary part of the evaluator's role [12, 30, 31]. These evaluators are likely to become advocates for their recommendations and enter into the political infighting necessary for implementation. Others, equally concerned with implementation of evaluation results, view implementation as a critical factor but one that is solely the responsibility of managers. They feel that evaluators who enter this political arena are operating on the manager's turf and may well decrease their credibility as evaluators. These authors hold that implementation of evaluation results is the responsibility of management. Evaluators who become advocates for their recommendations seldom consider the complexities of program management. Evaluation, even a good one, is only one management tool, and at best, it produces only one informational input into managerial decision making.

A third position is that a "middleman" role be developed to serve as a link between evaluators and managers [12, 32, 33]. The middleman role is similar to Reissman's "specialized bureaucrat" who maintains an interest in both his profession and the organization in which he is employed [34]. The role of middleman does not presently exist in most organizations, nor is it likely to emerge. Generic program management includes areas such as planning, evaluation, and decision making which are not easily extricable from each other. A major weakness is that ordinarily there are already too many organizational layers between the evaluator and the manager (see Chapter 5). Middlemen fill the role of qualified managers who blend a knowledge of program substance with information from evaluation studies and who are sensitive to the benefits obtainable from this approach. Ideally, this should be the manager because in the final analysis program managers must take the primary responsibility for utilization (or nonutilization) of evaluation [35].

The intent of many evaluation projects is implementation of evaluation results, and various strategies for effecting utilization have been proposed. In his review of these, Caro [10, 36] notes that many commentators stress close collaboration between evaluators and managers during each phase of the evaluation process. Greater involvement by managers in the evaluation process may increase their awareness of its potential contribution and increase the acceptability of evaluation results. Relevancy, timeliness, and clearly communicated findings are important factors in increasing potential implementation. Reporting in multiple forms, including "successive small-group feedback meetings from the top administrative level down through the ranks of subordinates to clarify interpretations and thus stimulate greater interest" contributes to the potential implementation of evaluation findings [10, 37].

Even under ideal conditions evaluators only *contribute* to the implementation of evaluation findings—the decision to implement or not remains the responsibility of managers.

Given the situational quality of program administration [38], the nonimplementation of evaluation results is apt to remain especially troublesome for evaluators whose criteria for successful evaluation is a program, modified by evaluation results. However, the manager who chooses *not* to implement modifications and changes suggested by evaluation should make some explanation or account as to why evaluation information is not reflected in his decisions and be prepared to defend that position.

MUTABLE TRUTHS. Given the methodological problems and the political aspects of evaluation, are we to conclude that good evaluation is, as yet, an unmet promise? Zusman and Bissonette [25] point out some of the factors that could lead to this conclusion.

1. Systematic, large-scale, sophisticated evaluation of most human service programs is too difficult and too expensive to be a realistic goal.
2. Good evaluations of many kinds of complex human service programs cannot be done at all, and in some cases should not be done.
3. Evaluations as currently conducted are likely to be poorly designed, underfunded, and forced on people unable or unwilling to implement them.
4. Evaluations, regardless of quality, are liable to be rejected, ignored, misinterpreted, or simply unnoticed.
5. Evaluations, when accepted, can be distorted as findings are incorporated into existing organizational patterns.
6. The design, conduct, and use of evaluations are always subject to valuational and political biases.
7. Resistance to evaluation will be present and multifaceted before, during, and after the effort.
8. With all other obstacles to evaluation removed, availability of research data will lag behind the exigencies of decision-making.

Widely touted as a panacea for ailing programs and a necessary component of all programs, evaluation consistently fails to produce results that achieve these expectations. Repeated failures tend to reinforce attitudes of undiluted pessimism concerning the utility of evaluation. However, evaluation can be, and increasingly is, a useful management tool and a viable practice for skilled personnel. The literature is perhaps too pessimistic concerning the contribution evaluation can make to program effectiveness. The question is not how to do away with evaluation but how to increase its utility for ongoing social programs. This leads us to a set of guidelines designed to accomplish this end.

SOME GUIDELINES FOR EVALUATION [12, 25].   *1. Evaluate if the results will have an effect on decisions.*   Programs should be considered negotiated structures that are not necessarily designed rationally; most evolve from vested interests of groups with sufficient power to initiate programs. Some programs evolve from default—federal monies are available, and programs are designed to spend the money by a certain deadline. Of course, a few social programs are consciously and rationally planned to impact on some target population; but even in these cases the gap between the problem that is to be alleviated by the program and the capabilities of the program is often great simply because not enough is known about many social problems or how to design programs that are adequate for the purpose.

The mistaken assumption that all programs can and should be evaluated results in much wasted effort and contributes to the attitude that evaluation has no utility. How much evaluation can add is limited if many similar programs have been evaluated and the factors that lead to increased effectiveness are known but not adopted.

Before evaluation, evaluators and practitioners should agree on the definition of the problem, acceptable models, data, and techniques to be used, and how the results are to be used.

2. Evaluate programs that are amenable to change in response to evaluation.   The image of an open dynamic program with managers who seek objective information and adapt to feedback is not totally accurate. Well-established programs are somewhat rigid; are enmeshed in networks of alliances with other programs; are governed by rules, regulations, and laws; and have survived many threats to their continued existence. Structural constraints, power patterns, vested interests in the status quo, inter- and intraorganizational alliances, annual budgets, and bureaucratic forms of organization are only a few of the factors that produce inertia and decrease responsiveness to even the most prevailing justifications for change.

The institutionalization of the ability to respond to evaluation is a long and difficult process requiring sometimes radical changes in existing programs. The emerging approaches to evaluation (Chapter 3) are attempts to provide mechanisms to increase a program's ability to respond and information upon which to base decisions to change.

Some authors suggest that programs be evaluated "early, before vested interests have solidified and organizational inertia has set in." Wholey [39:21] recommends early evaluation because of the paucity of theories that allow accurate prediction of the outcome of program activities. Early evaluation can supply necessary information to program managers so they can redirect program activities toward program goals. This is sound advice, but it is not always feasible. Because evaluation is far from a standardized procedure, it can be tailored to impact on well-established as well as new programs, but evaluators must use all of their political and scientific skills in the long and difficult process of negotiating to achieve a consensual basis for change.

3. *Evaluate only if the probability of producing valid, precise, and applicable information is high.* Given methodological and political constraints, not all programs can be or should be evaluated. The advice given students of survey

research—bite less and chew more [40]—is especially appropriate for evaluators and agencies that fund evaluation studies. Funds for evaluation are usually attached to new human service programs, and it is easy to be seduced into evaluating them without regard for the quality of evaluation simply because funds are available. In addition, many programs are designed to impact on major problems when we know very little about *how* to solve these problems. The rationale here is that something is better than nothing, but to evaluate a program's impact on a target population seems fruitless if there are strong reasons to suggest that the program has no impact. In such instances "subjective" evaluation is probably an adequate basis for trying new programs.

4. *Evaluation results must be made conceptually clear to program administrators, managers, and practitioners.* Evaluation cannot be used by program personnel unless they understand the results. For example, complex generalizations developed from elegant regression equations may be methodologically sound information but have little or no meaning for program personnel. Greatly simplified and properly translated from precise formulations into the somewhat more sloppy but more understandable language of the world of action, evaluation results are more likely to be accepted by program personnel. This does not imply that evaluation results should be made less valid and precise—only that they be transmitted in a language understandable to program personnel.

Learning the language of program managers is helpful. Because a variety of program managers and programs at various levels may be involved, the language of particular program managers must be learned.

Evaluation results should reflect the needs of program

managers and recommendations should focus on changes that can be made by program managers.

Use of both formal and informal mechanisms to disseminate evaluation results to program managers may increase the likelihood of acceptance. But the method of dissemination should be negotiated prior to the evaluation project.

The Potential of Evaluation.   Many of the programs aimed at reducing, controlling, or ameliorating certain aspects of visible and costly social problems are designed under the assumption that certain program activities will ameliorate certain social problems. They are undertaken without a great deal of knowledge about the relationships between program activities and program impact [39:20]. Programs then fail to deliver according to expectations, not necessarily from a lack of effort or resources, but from a lack of knowledge about the most effective techniques of intervention. At the risk of being overly idealistic, we suggest that evaluation, by achieving a delicate balance between scientific canons and applied results, can indicate the effectiveness of public service programs. By isolating the effects of program activities and pointing out those activities most effective in ameliorating social problems, evaluation can also provide information on wasted efforts and ineffectual techniques, and this information can be used to redirect program activities. Thus, evaluation can build a body of knowledge applicable to improving the techniques of intervention.

We are not suggesting that any one evaluation project adds significantly to this body of knowledge, nor are we touting evaluation as a cure-all for social ills. Our claim is more modest: Evaluation makes possible more objective decisions about program design and operation and the allocation of resources by providing accurate assessments of the economic and social costs and benefits of a program [39]. In this sense evaluation is an emerging discipline, combining the systematic analytical approach of scientific inquiry with an understanding of program processes, which has the potential of providing a more adequate basis for decisions regarding programs than is presently available from other sources [12:128; 41:126].

The limitations of evaluations should be recognized, but its potential, as a management tool, to improve effectiveness and to explicate the important effects of a program makes the effort involved in overcoming these limitations worthwhile.

SOME CONCLUDING REMARKS. Many commentators [37, 14, 42] have pointed to the seemingly poor track record of program evaluation and evaluative research, emphasizing that evaluation commonly fails to affect program policymaking or program administration. For those who measure evaluation in terms of its contribution to the effectiveness of ongoing programs, evaluation has, for the most part, failed to deliver. Ironically, evaluation is a management tool that can provide valid, precise, and applicable information; but unless managers use this information for decision making purposes, evaluation becomes an unprofitable activity for management. This does not mean that evaluation fails if it does not affect program activities—only that it fails if it is not considered, along with other information, by program managers as a basis for decision making.

The most powerful contribution of evaluation to program

effectiveness is information that meets the criteria of scientific inquiry and is timely, relevant, and applicable. Whether this information is used by managers as a basis for decision making is another issue, commonly outside the evaluator's area of control. The implementation of evaluation findings is a critical issue which will influence the future conduct of evaluation activities. But to insist that the ultimate criterion of "good" evaluation is the extent to which it results in effective programs is specious, at least as it implies that the implementation of evaluation findings is the responsibility of evaluators.

REFERENCES

1. Carol H. Weiss, "Between the Cup and the Lip," *Evaluation,* I, 49–55 (#2, 1973).
2. Edward A. Suchman, *Evaluative Research,* Russell Sage Foundation, New York, 1967.
3. Walter Williams, "The Capacity of Social Science Organization to Perform Large-Scale Evaluative Research," Public Policy Paper No. 2, Institute of Government, University of Washington, 1971.
4. Saul Feldman, "Problems and Prospects: Administration in Mental Health," *Administration in Mental Health,* I, 4–11 (Winter, 1972).
5. Bernard Gifford, "Policy Analysis and the City," *Evaluation,* I, 27–30 (#3, 1973).
6. Jack Zusman and Eleanor Ross, "Evaluation of the Quality of Mental Health Services," *Archives of General Psychiatry,* XX, 352 (March 1969).
7. Leland H. Towle et al., *Alcoholism Program Program Monitoring System Development—Evaluation of the ATC Program* (HSM-42-71-115), Sanford Research Institute, March 1973.
8. Joseph S. Wholey and Bayla White, "Evaluation's Impact on Title I Elementary and Secondary Education Program Management," *Evaluation,* I, 73–76 (#3, 1973).
9. Garth Buchanan, Pamela Horst, and John Scanlon, "Improving Federal Evaluation Planning," *Evaluation,* I, 86–90 (#2, 1973).

10. Francis G. Caro, "Approaches to Evaluative Research: A Review," *Human Organization,* XXVIII, 87–99 (Summer 1969).

11. Michael Scriven, "The Methodology of Evaluation," in Ralph W. Tyler et al. (eds.), *Perspectives of Curriculum Evaluation,* Rand McNally, Chicago, 1967, pp. 39–83.

12. Carol H. Weiss, *Evaluation Research,* Prentice-Hall, Englewood Cliffs, N.J., 1972.

13. Walter Williams, *The Capacity of Social Science Organizations to Perform Large Scale Evaluation Research,* Institute of Governmental Research, University of Washington, Seattle, 1971.

14. Thomas A. Morehouse, "Program Evaluation: Social Research Versus Public Policy," *Public Administration Review* (November/December 1972).

15. Delbert C. Miller, "The Shaping of Research Design in Large-Scale Group Research," *Social Forces,* XXXIII, 383–390 (May 1955). Excerpts are from Delbert C. Miller, *Handbook of Research Design & Social Measurement,* 2nd ed., David McKay, New York, 1970, pp. 43, 50.

16. James Coleman, *Policy Research in the Social Sciences,* General Learning Corporation, Morristown, N.J., 1972.

17. L. Dave Brown, "Research Action: Organizational Feedback, Understanding, and Change," *The Journal of Applied Behavioral Science,* VIII, 697–711 (#6, 1972).

18. Chris Argyris, *The Applicability of Organizational Sociology,* Cambridge University Press, 1972.

19. Roy J. Lewicki and Clayton P. Alderfer, "The Tensions Between Research and Intervention in Intergroup Conflict," *The Journal of Applied Behavioral Science,* IX, 423–468 (#4, 1973).

20. Caro, Francis G., "Integration of Evaluative Research and Social Planning Roles: A Case Study," *Human Organization,* XXXIII, 351–358 (#4, 1974).

21. Carol H. Weiss, "Where Politics and Evaluation Research Meet," *Evaluation,* I, 37–45 (#3, 1973).

22. P. W. Bridgeman, "New Vistas for Intelligence," in E. P. Wigner, ed., *Physical Science and Human Values,* Princeton University Press, Princeton, N.J., 1947.

23. Emile Durkheim, *The Rules of Sociological Method,* Free Press, New York, 1938.

24. Curtis G. Southard, *Symposium on the Evaluation of Community Mental Health Programs,* National Institute of Mental Health, Washington, D.C., 1952–53. Reported in Edward A. Suchman, "A Model for Research and Evaluation on Rehabilitation," in *Sociology and Rehabilitation,* Marvin Sussman, ed., American Sociological Association, Washington, D.C. 1965, 52–70.

25. Jack Zusman and Raymond Bissonette, "The Case Against Evaluation," *International Journal of Mental Health*, II, 111–125 (Summer 1973).

26. Donald T. Campbell, "Reforms as Experiments," *American Psychologist*, XXIV, 409–429 (April 1969).

27. Howard R. Davis, "Four Ways to Goal Attainment: An Overview," *Evaluation*, Special Monograph #1, 23–28 (1973).

28. Selma J. Mushkin, "Evaluation: Use With Caution," *Evaluation*, I, 31–35 (#2, 1973).

29. *Executive Summary, Design of an Evaluation System for the National Institute of Mental Health* (Project #72-1), The Urban Institute, Washington, D.C., February 1973. The quotations are from NIMH's evaluation of the project.

30. Robert Longwood and Arnold Simmel, "Organizational Resistance to Innovation Suggested by Research," in *Evaluating Action Programs: Readings in Social Action and Education*, Carol H. Weiss, ed., Allyn and Bacon, Boston, 1972, pp. 311–317.

31. Chris Argyris, "Creating Effective Research Relationships in Organizations," *Human Organization*, XVII, 38–40 (#1, 1958).

32. Ronald G. Havelock, "Dissemination and Translation Roles," in *Knowledge Production and Utilization in Educational Administration*, Terry L. Eidell and Joanne M. Kitchel, eds., Eugene, Oregon, Center for the Advanced Study of Educational Administration, 1968, pp. 64–119.

33. William Kornhauser, *Scientists in Industry*, University of California Press, Berkeley, Calif., 1961.

34. Leonard Reissman, "A Study of Role Conception in Bureaucracy," *Social Forces*, XXVII, 305–310 (1949).

35. Toni Tripodi, Phillip Fellin, and Irwin Epstein, *Social Program Evaluation: Guidelines for Health, Education and Welfare Administrators*, F. E. Peacock Publishers, Itasca, Ill., 1971, p. 137.

36. Chris Argyris, "Creating Effective Relationships in Organizations," in R. Adams and J. Preiss, eds., *Human Organization Research*, Dorsey Press, Homewood, Ill., 1960, pp. 109–123.

37. Floyd Mann and Renis Likert, "The Need for Research on the Communication of Research Results," in R. Adams and J. Preiss, eds., *Human Organization Research*, Dorsey Press, Homewood, Ill., 1960, pp. 57–66.

38. Saul Feldman, "Problems and Prospects: Administration in Mental Health," *Administration in Mental Health*, 10 (Winter 1973).

39. Joseph S. Wholey et al., *Federal Evaluation Policy: Analyzing the Effects of Public Programs*, Washington, D.C., The Urban Institute, 1970.

40. James A. Davis, *Elementary Survey Analysis,* Prentice-Hall, Englewood Cliffs, N.J., 1971, p. 186.

41. Harry P. Hatry, Richard E. Winnie, and Donald M. Fisk, *Practical Program Evaluation for State and Local Government Officials,* Washington, D.C., The Urban Institute, 1973.

42. Walter Williams and John Evans, "The Politics of Evaluation: The Case of Head Start," *The Annals,* 385, 118–132 (September 1969).

5
Evaluation and Management

In the first four chapters we have addressed evaluation from two perspectives: 1) historical emergence and current evolution and 2) the evaluator and his decisions, contexts, methods, and problems. The terms *management responsibility, management subspecialty, management decision making, arm of management, managers and practitioners,* and so on, have been used frequently and sometimes casually, but the primary perspective has been that of the evaluator who is ultimately responsible for the actual conduct of these activities and the communication of insights and implications. In this chapter the focus is shifted somewhat to that of the manager or to management generically. Specifically, we examine the evaluation function within the context of coordinated management of complex organizations. We "replow" some of the ground covered, or at least prepared, earlier—we hope from a new perspective. This is a treatise on evaluation, however, not on management; so although the perspective and framework of presentation are those of management, the central concern and points of elaboration are those of program evaluation. First is a brief discussion of the organizational placement of evaluation responsibility—a problem that, probably more than any other, has caused real controversy because it involves organizational power and territoriality. The next part of the chapter is a typology of evaluation activities that roughly parallels a temporal model of organizational activity and managerial decision making. The chapter ends with a discussion relating evaluation to other management functions.

Two assumptions, which have implicitly and explicitly guided the presentation in the first four chapters, are worth repeating in the context of evaluation as a management function.

1. The responsibility for program evaluation lies with the manager of the program. Although the manager need not personally conduct evaluations, his responsibility is to see that it is done, and done in such a way as to assist him in the areas of improved service delivery and accountability.

2. The most reliable and powerful approaches to program evaluation are those that utilize some of the rigors of research methodology. However, the characteristics program evaluation must *always* and *without fail* share with science are not specific methodologies and techniques of research but, rather, *an uncompromising impartiality and a clear and logical progression from evidence to conclusion.*

THE ORGANIZATIONAL PLACEMENT OF EVALUATION.

The question of the organizational locus of evaluation has been prominent for as long as program evaluation has been discussed as a specialized management function. Usually, the problem is voiced as a dispute between the relative merits and demerits of having evaluation—and the evaluator—"inside" or "outside" the program being evaluated. For such a debate to have the history that it does, there must be strong and valid arguments for each position.

One perplexing question in the discussion of internal-versus-external evaluation is a clear delineation of what is meant by *internal* and what is meant by *external*—or more bluntly, "internal or external to what?" The most useful way to discuss this problem is to conceptualize programs and organizations as social systems composed of interacting subunits that are at the same time interacting elements of a suprasystem. The question of internal or external evaluation then becomes one of the appropriate systems level for the evaluator. If evaluation is seen as a component or subcomponent of the system level being evaluated, evaluation is considered *internal*. If evaluation or the evaluator is seen as a representative of a part of the system not "managed" by the element being evaluated, the evaluation is seen as *external*.

Internal and *external* are treated here, as they are treated in most of the literature, *as if* they were dichotomous, when in fact they are extremes of a continuum. The format of this chapter retains the usual dichotomy, but the discussion touches many points along the external-internal *continuum*. The concept of systems levels is discussed more thoroughly later in the chapter, but the point should be made here that those who disagree about the locus of evaluation activity agree that evaluation is a legitimate and necessary managerial function. We should also note that those qualities that are usually seen as strengths of one locus are seen as the weaknesses of the other.

External Evaluation.   Can an evaluator who is part of the system being evaluated be "objective"? A person who is a member of the program being evaluated, so the argument goes, is "too close" to the program and its participants and because of pride, loyalty, or job security will not be able to be objective in assessing strengths and limitations, effectiveness and ineffectiveness, and so on. This argument tends to be particularly pointed when directed to a program manager. Although the argument is usually phrased in terms of objectivity, it tends to obscure the issue, because objectivity is usually considered a quality of a person rather than an organization. Certainly an internal evaluator can be just as objective as one external to the program. A more important question is one of credibility—or where should the evaluator be located so that his evaluations and findings will be believed by the widest circle of potential decision makers? Internal evaluations are often suspect to those representing or comprising suprasystems. The major argument in favor of external evaluation, then, is its credibility, which is a characteristic of systems and not of the evaluator or the manager.

This discussion vastly oversimplifies the complex issues of objectivity. The term *objectivity* itself has multiple meanings in the general vocabulary, meanings that differ somewhat from the more specialized connotations of the scientific vocabulary. One connotation the authors wish to avoid is the equation of *objective* with *good*. Regardless of the organizational locus of formal program evaluation, the activity may be done well or badly, and objectivity is only one possible confounding issue.

The "internal" evaluator may have his objectivity sorely tried—the age-old problem of distinguishing forests and trees. The point to be made here is that much of what parades under the banner of "objectivity" is really a question of credibility—a confusion that tends to complicate rational decision making in the area of program evaluation. Several degrees of "internalness" and "externalness" are discussed in the next section.

Internal Evaluation. The major argument in favor of internal evaluation, and the major weakness seen in external evaluation, lie in the evaluator's knowledge of the program, its history and circumstances, which is necessary for a balanced, in-depth, and "objective" evaluation. Thus, "objectivity" is also the major argument in favor of internal evaluation, but whereas external evaluation equates *objective* with distance, internal evaluation equates *objective* with depth of knowledge, or "the nature of reality." External evaluators usually must start their work with limited, if any, knowledge of the program. The results of external evaluation, while credible to the suprasystem, frequently tell program managers little or nothing they did not already know, and therefore it lacks utility to the program being evaluated and cannot inform decision makers. This problem is treated further in the discussion of differing needs for evaluation.

The major argument in favor of external evaluation is its

credibility, and the major argument in favor of internal evaluation is its utility. All of these considerations bear on the question of the proper organizational placement of the evaluator, a topic we discuss after exploring some other dimensions. To anticipate the discussion slightly, we believe that the evaluation staff can be located inside the larger system but outside the program to be evaluated. This arrangement has all of the advantages and none of the disadvantages of truly outside evaluation, and at the same time it avoids the disadvantages of the extreme "internal" evaluation.

Contractual evaluation illustrates the continuous nature of "internal" and "external" evaluation. It may take the form of management contracting with an outside organization to examine a program or a system, to make judgments about it and recommendations for it; or an evaluator contracting for a particular piece of work to be done—either a particular evaluation, the development of instruments, the demonstration of techniques, or the acceleration of the implementation of an evaluation system. In any case it represents the expenditure of resources to others for a product or service over which the contracting organization has no control, except possibly for certain sanctions in the case of nonperformance. Those doing the evaluation are assumed to have no vested interest in the program and to possess greater expertise than do program personnel. While this is usually true, these people frequently are unclear about the purposes of the evaluation and do not question the relevance of their skills to the evaluation problem. The result is often disappointing in that the purchasers find the product or service poorly done or largely irrelevant to the intended purposes [1].

Contractual evaluation has become one major activity of

management consulting firms, which have long been a part of the corporate scenery. Typically, these organizations began as accounting firms which performed the annual external audits required of public corporations and organizations holding public charters. For many, their functions expanded to include an advisory capacity for all aspects of management, and, especially since the 1950s, program evaluation. The proliferation of such firms attests to the demand for such services but also makes the term *management consultant firm* fairly nonspecific, encompassing a range of organizations from a few that are multinational corporations to large numbers that are secondary or sideline occupations for persons with other primary employment. Another type of organization that has recently become heavily involved in contract evaluation is the private research organization. Several such organizations were formed specifically to respond to requests for proposals, including those dealing with program evaluation. Outside the area of program evaluation, there is little overlap in the activities of these two types of organizations. The fact that they overlap in the area of program evaluation is a reflection of the dual origin of evaluation as a subspecialty.

At the other extreme of contractual evaluation, an organization may contract with a constituent unit to perform internal evaluation. This arrangement tends to minimize the internal-external dilemma because the program or component can maximize the utility of the evaluation activity and at the same time the contracting level of the organization can exercise sufficient surveillance and control to ensure the quality, comparability, and credibility of the effort. This infers, of course, that the contractee has the necessary skills and commitment and that the contractor actually does monitor the process. One composite arrangement that has shown some promise is for evaluations to be designed at a system or top management level, and then constituent subunits are contracted for its implementation. This method tends to blur the internal-external dichotomy and may increase the receptivity of programs to evaluation results, although the evaluations are of uneven quality.

There are, of course, many forms of contractual evaluation falling on a continuum between these extremes. What is highlighted by both contractual evaluation and the relationship of evaluation to management are the dual problems of autonomy and accountability as they apply to program evaluation. Because of its specialized and sometimes sensitive nature, its close identification with the control function of management, the political utilization to which it is often subjected, and the questions of credibility, evaluation and evaluators must maintain a degree of autonomy much greater than that required by any other support or management staff function. The autonomy of the evaluator is best assured in contractual evaluation in its most common forms, because once the contract is made, the contractor has little or no control over the activities of the contractee.

Another part of the basic dilemma is that of accountability for evaluation. If the evaluator is a part of the organization, questions of accountability are usually easily resolved. In the case of contractual evaluation, however, accountability becomes problematic. With the signing of the contract, the organization usually surrenders all responsibility for the quality and utility of the evaluation— in fact, freedom from such responsibility is one major motivation for the contract. However, the nature of accountability dictates that, once established, it cannot be delegated elsewhere, much less contracted. Therefore, the manager or the organization doing the contracting remains accountable for the quality and utility of a product over which he has almost no control.

Controversy about the proper organizational placement of evaluation has also arisen from a failure to find satisfactory answers to the question "evaluation for whom?" This question is a result of misunderstanding the nature of evaluation and treating it as a unitary entity. Most of the published literature on evaluation tends to treat it as primarily an information-*generating* process. Such a definition is only partly true—evaluation is also an information-*weighing* process. Obviously, for information to be utilized it must first be reliably generated, but that activity is secondary to and supportive of the weighing process. For as long as individuals and social entities have been making interventions and exercising power, those persons have been making judgments about the impact and efficacy of their interventions. Only recently have individuals and collectivities become concerned about systematizing the judgmental process and with holding other individuals and collectivities accountable for the effects of their interventions. Among the results of these changing public sensitivities have been an increased concern with the nature, source, and reliability of information; the subsequent emergence of evaluation as a management subspecialty, largely concerned with the generation and presentation of information; and a tendency to confuse the relationship of information generation and information weighing to decision making.

Because, in social programs, interventions are made at all levels—from individual practitioners, through several layers of management, to the highest policymaker—all have need of evaluation, and most, given the nature of modern management, need trained evaluators. At each level the nature of the decisions to be made differ, and therefore the information needs at each level differ. Although such a statement seems idiotically simplistic, the nature of evaluation is so poorly understood, the term is so popular, and so many activities parade under the evaluation label, many people believe that "evaluation" or "doing an evaluation" will somehow, almost mystically, solve the information needs of all levels. There are several very realistic contributors to this problem. Systematic, or formal, evaluation (in the sense of generating information) is expensive, and trained evaluators are few. Therefore, managers and evaluators attempt to load as much as possible into one formal evaluation effort. Unfortunately, the time required to complete the effort is increased, thus decreasing the timeliness of the information, and much of the information generated is not useful to any given level. Even when evaluation efforts are kept to a reasonably modest scale, the assumption is pervasive that the information needed at one level of management is, or should be, relevant at all other levels. Because resources devoted to formal evaluation are usually limited, these issues become important in determining the organizational placement of evaluation capabilities.

In summary, for evaluation to have impact, it must be credible; for that impact to be constructive, evaluation must be informed and in some depth. To be credible, the evaluator must enjoy considerable autonomy, but to optimize impact, the manager must exercise his control function. There are some realistic contradictions implied in the above statements, and the organizational dilemma becomes one of finding the optimal compromise. All managers evaluate their programs, but these methods of evaluating are no longer considered sufficient. Special skills and special information are needed. Ideally, these special evaluation skills would be available to every managerial level, but available resources often prohibit such a solution. Usually some kind of decision is required about where in an organizational structure specialized evaluation capabilities are to be placed, given the considerations of credibility and utility and assuming that a decision has been made not to rely solely upon contractual evaluation.

For human service programs, the highest organizational level having responsibility and accountability for the direct delivery of services appears appropriate for specialized evaluation capabilities. Program evaluation would be available to all programs within the organization, but the evaluation agency would not be accountable to program managers. While this does not resolve the dilemmas noted, it does minimize them. It places evaluation close enough to service delivery and practicing professionals to permit in-depth knowledge of events and conditions that have shaped programs as well as familiarity with the current constraints and idiosyncratic factors impinging upon program managers. At the same time, the evaluation agency is sufficiently "distant" to be credible in all but a very few instances. This arrangement limits the need for "imported external" evaluation to those rare instances in which the credibility of top management is itself suspect or to those occasions requiring one-shot evaluations of such scope as to necessitate, but not warrant, the considerable expansion of permanent evaluation personnel. By placing evaluation clearly within the structure of accountability and making the evaluator responsible to the top manager, evaluation as a management function is underscored and the administrative control of evaluation is more clearly specified. While only a secure and comfortable administrator can assure the necessary autonomy, this arrangement does free the evaluator somewhat from the uncertain and sometimes covert demands and motivations of political officeholders and program managers within the system.

When responsibility for evaluation is placed at a lower organizational level, problems of credibility and expense multiply. Unless evaluation can be built into a routine record keeping and reporting system, the quality is often not appreciably higher than the unaided expert judgment of the program manager. If the responsibility for evaluation is placed higher in the organizational sequence of systems (i.e., those that have exclusively administrative, coordinative, and policy responsibilities and are outside the accountability structure for the delivery of services) a knowledge of, and appreciation for, the enormous "real-world" complexities facing human service programs tend to be missing. In such instances evaluation often is reduced to concerns of economy and effort (the cheapest is the best) or unrealistic demands are placed upon managers. This is not to deny the very real need of persons at these higher levels and at legislative levels for policy analysis, which may be a form of program evaluation.

This is not an ideal solution, only a viable compromise. The ideal is probably continuous monitoring, but no process incorporating evaluation has yet been successfully implemented.

While evaluation should not be divorced from the system of program delivery (although managers of social programs are often less than enthusiastic about this function) most service delivery systems are not equipped to address certain specialized tasks. For example, the development of new evaluation techniques and methodologies, particularly in the conceptually and methodologically difficult areas of program impacts, would appear to be a natural challenge for university-based researchers and quite consonant with their historical and traditional role. However, universities have not responded to this challenge and have tended to engage in traditional research activities under the guise of evaluation. Coordination and dissemination of evaluation-related knowledge would seem to be a natural function for evaluation agencies at the federal government level, but like the universities, these agencies have not defined their roles primarily in these terms.

In summary, the tasks and challenges of program evaluation require a considerable range of expertise and differentiation of roles. We suggest one possible distribution of tasks.

THE PROGRAM MATRIX, PROGRAM EVALUATION, AND SYSTEMS. This discussion is intended to build upon the systems model of program evaluation. Some of the management problems are indicated, some concepts of system/subsystem/suprasystem interaction are introduced.

General systems theory and its various derivatives have had a tremendous impact upon management; so in evaluation, and management generally we speak of systems (the focal point at any given time), subsystems (the constituent units of the system), and suprasystems (the larger context of which the focal system is a constituent unit). Any given set of activities may be a system, subsystem, or suprasystem, depending upon the perspective from which it is being viewed.

These distinctions, although wholly conceptual, are useful in minimizing confusion about the point and purpose of evaluation activities and in tracing and understanding the sources and consequences of change at multiple organizational levels. For managers to know where change will have the greatest impact is sometimes important so that steps can be taken to minimize disruption. For instance, the manager of a focal system may bring about enormous changes in the subsystems under his jurisdiction without seriously compromising the integrity of the system itself, if potentially disruptive impacts can be closely monitored and resulting administrative, morale, or other problems quickly addressed. However, relatively small changes that have a disruptive or threatening impact upon the suprasystem (and, by definition, the manager's superordinates) can, and frequently do, have a calamitous effect upon the focal system and the career of the manager. As a matter of practice, the role of the evaluator may be to perform the postmortem (the term *social system pathologist* has been used) and there are those who feel that this is the appropriate role for the evaluator.* However, the evaluator, by having a thorough knowledge of the system in which he is working, can be used to predict and cushion the effects of change and thus become a social systems clinician.

The systems terminology of input-processor-output

---

* At a meeting of a task force on the scope and functions of program evaluation, convened by the Southern Regional Education Board, some participants expressed surprise to learn that there were any *other* functions.

model provides one simple but useful way to conceptualize a service delivery system (see Figure 5.1).

This general schematic representation can be used to describe any system capable of self-correction but is used here only as a means of differentiating and discussing varieties of program evaluation within human service organizations. The basic assumption is that the organization, here called the "processor," is designed to bring about some change, in this instance to meet some need or to alleviate an undesirable condition. To accomplish this, there are certain inputs; financial and personnel resources, clients, information; and so on. These inputs are "processed" in ways designed to accomplish the purposes of the organization, the results being the organization's outputs. For an organization to be self-maintaining and self-correcting, feedback information about how well the organization is performing is necessary. Based partially on this feedback, decisions are made about maintaining or altering the amount and kind of input, the nature of the processing activities, or both. All of this takes place within an organizational environment that consists not only of the various levels of the suprasystem but also the population, which has some unmet needs or undesirable conditions the organization is designed to meet or alleviate.

This framework is used in the present context only as a paradigm for categorizing types of evaluation activities and

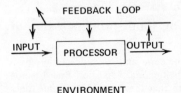

Figure 5.1.   Schematic representation of a system.

indicating how these activities can be used by management. Rather than distinct categories, this paradigm should be viewed as a useful classificatory device. These classifications are based on the assumption that an entire evaluation system is operational. As was stated in the definition, some of these activities would not be considered evaluative unless they contribute to an understanding of the organization's output or impact.

Input Evaluation.   There are two types of input evaluation: needs assessment and the evaluation of effort. Needs assessment refers to any of the variety of methods used to gauge the state of the population relative to the services offered. It is directed toward the organizational environment. The evaluation of effort is concerned with the program itself, particularly that constellation of resources and clients represented by the "input" arrow in Figure 5.1.

Effort Evaluation.   Usually routinized into statistical systems and budget justifications, effort evaluation consists of enumerating clients receiving services, types of services rendered, staff time expenditures, how funds are expended—in short, the extent and type of program effort. As Suchman states:

> Evaluations in this category have as their criterion of success the quantity and quality of activity that takes place. This represents an assessment of input or energy regardless of output. It is intended to answer the question "What did you do" and "How well did you do it?" [2:61]

He goes on to compare this type of evaluation to the "measurement of the number of times a bird flaps his wings without any attempt to determine how far the bird has flown" [2:61]. Effort evaluation is useful, however, for assessing the utilization of resources in terms of program priorities and for increasing the efficiency of effort. For instance, programs often inadvertently fall into patterns of operations that are at variance with their expressed intents—inordinate amounts of traveling, an emphasis on direct services to the neglect of preventive activities (or some other combination of overemphasis and neglect), or other patterns that may be easily corrected once they become visible.

Effort evaluation is also useful for monitoring changes in the demand for services, thus revealing needed alterations in resource allocation; it can signal a marked increase in the number of a particular category of clients coming for services so that the program can be maximally responsive to the demands for it. Effort evaluation is also useful in explaining the program activities to the suprasystem, including funding sources. Such justification is greatly strengthened when used in combination with other kinds of evaluation, but it can certainly be assumed that in the absence of effort, little good is being accomplished. Some maintain that effort evaluation is not a legitimate activity for program evaluators. Certainly, if effort information exists through some other established organizational activity— statistical reporting systems, work/time studies, budget narratives, or whatever—it should not be duplicated by the evaluator. However, the evaluator might be concerned with alternative sources of information because such information is a part of an integrated and comprehensive evaluation scheme and is immediately useful to the program manager. The evaluator might have to interpret or clarify the program implications of effort indicators and indicate how they are related to outcome.

Another way in which the term *input* is used in program evaluation involves the types of variables used in the various research techniques discussed in Chapter 3. Weiss [3:45–47] distinguishes two types of input variables: those having to do with the characteristics of the program, such as purpose, methods, staffing, size of program, and management; and those descriptive of clients, such as demographic characteristics, attitudes, motivations, and expectations. She also points out two reasons why such variables are important—they clarify the meaning and dimensions of the program, and they contribute to an understanding of the differential effects of various program elements.

Needs Assessment.   One activity in which the management concerns of planning and evaluation overlap is needs assessment (see Fig. 5.2). The approaches to needs assessment vary widely in terms of precision, difficulty, and expense. The choice of an approach will be dictated by the requirements of the situation and the time and resources available. The following discussion follows that of Warheit, Bell, and Schwab [4]. Although originally presented in terms of mental health needs assessment, it is equally applicable to other human service areas. Needs assessment is an important planning activity, quite apart from its contribution to evaluation. If needs assessment is to be used as an evaluative device, however, the approach that will be most amenable to the later assessment of impact should be chosen. To be useful as a program evaluation tool, needs must be assessed at more than one point in time.

1.   The key informant approach, as the name implies, "is based on information secured from those in the area who are in a good position to know what the community's needs and utilization patterns are" [4:28]. It is widely and successfully used within the field of anthropology and has the distinct advantage of being relatively simple and inexpensive. In the context of needs assessment, it may have the added advantages of fostering community discussion, initiating or strengthening interaction among representatives of diverse community interests, and cementing or documenting community support. The major disadvantage is that this approach tends to rely on community and agency leaders, most of whom already have formed conclusions about "community needs" and who, by definition, do not represent those "invisible populations" frequently most in need of services and assistance. Although frequently practiced it is a difficult technique to translate reliably and validly into program evaluation. Programs that rely upon boards and advisory groups to assess the fit between programs and needs and progress in meeting needs rely on groups of picked key informants. The quality and representativeness of the board or advisory group determine the quality of the evaluation, but in almost no case can program accomplishments be documented. Boards and advisory groups can be of enormous assistance in encouraging the provision of adequate evaluation information; but their record as technical evaluators is not to be envied.

2.   The community forum approach is essentially an extension of the key informant approach but overcomes at

least one major disadvantage of the former by broadening representation to include the general public. The central technique of this approach is one or a number of public meetings to which all residents are invited and at which all views are solicited. With the rise of consumerism, the crucial importance of consumer input increasingly has been explicitly recognized, sometimes legislatively. Like the previous approach, the major advantages of the community forum approach are the relative ease and economy of public meetings and the relatively broad representation. One major disadvantage of this approach is assuring adequate representation. The community forum is not a familiar or comfortable vehicle of expression for all subpopulations, and there is a real danger that crucial needs may go unrecognized. A concomitant danger is that the meetings may be dominated by groups or subpopulations seeking only to air grievances or to use such meetings for the establishment of a power base. Certain logistical problems, such as appropriate meeting sites and times, may increase in larger communities. Despite these shortcomings, the community forum is an important mechanism for soliciting community interest and solidifying community support. Like the key informant approach, however, it is extremely difficult to translate such assessments into program evaluation, although previously unconsidered evaluative variables may come to light.

3. The rates under treatment approach approach is an attempt to overcome some of the biases inherent in the impressionism of the first two approaches. Basically, this approach is used to make some estimates or statements about persons in need of services based on the enumeration and characteristics of persons receiving services. In the field of

mental health at least, this approach has a long history in studies of prevalence and the distribution of treatment [5, 6]. The major advantages lie in the fairly easy accessibility of data and the ease and economy of its analysis.

Despite its strengths and its admitted utility in understanding the operation of a current delivery system, it has some distinct disadvantages as a needs assessment approach to be utilized in either planning or evaluation. These disadvantages center around how to use the data. To translate rates under treatment into needs assessment for planning or evaluation, it seems necessary to make one of two assumptions, both of which are false. Rates under treatment are used to identify and describe those receiving services which, when compared to the characteristics of the total population, yields a description of those "not served." The purpose of this exercise, presumably, is to plan and develop programs to reach the unserved populations. However, this is based on the assumption that the unmet need or undesirable condition is uniformly distributed throughout the population. Field research has shown that this is not true. If rates under treatment are to be used in planning or evaluation, it must be assumed that those receiving treatment at any given time are randomly drawn from the population in need of services and therefore accurately reflect the population. This assumption also is contradicted by research evidence.

In summary, rates under treatment is at best precarious and should be used in planning only with extreme caution. As a part of the evaluation of effort, however, and as an element of continuous monitoring, *but only when used in combination with other kinds of information,* rates under treatment have proved to be of some utility.

4.   The social indicator approach as an evaluation tool is discussed in some detail under impact evaluation. It is sufficient to note here that social indicators have long been used in needs assessment. Basically, the technique consists of making inferences about a population, based on various kinds of descriptive statistics that are assumed or known to be indirect measures or correlates of the need or condition of interest. Warheit et al. [4:47] list as the most common indicators: the sociodemographic characteristics of the population; the social ecology of the community; patterns of social behavior, such as crime rates, substance abuse, family patterns, and so on; and the general living and economic conditions, such as unemployment, housing, accessibility to services, and so on.

Frequently, the use of social indicators is informal, almost casual, but a number of fairly rigorous techniques do exist to guide the planner in his inferences, probably the best known and most widely used of which is social area analysis. [7, 8] Social indicator analysis has so far been far more useful for planning than for evaluation. It has the distinct advantage of utilizing a wide range of fairly readily available statistics, which can be secured fairly economically. In addition, it is an extremely flexible approach encompassing such a range of rigor as to suit almost any specific planning requirement. The major disadvantages, in addition to those discussed below, lie in the fact that it is inferential, and statements cannot be made about the characteristics of individuals within an area based on the rates or averages for the area. In short, without extreme caution it is easy to get into the ecological fallacy [9, 10].

5.   The survey approach assesses the needs of a population based on a sample of the entire population and relies

upon the responses of those in the sample to reflect accurately their conditions and positions and, by generalization, those of the population. Surveys are a familiar part of the American scene, and there are many fine volumes on the techniques of sample surveys (see Chapter 3). Sample surveys are the most satisfactory form of needs assessment, from the point of view of evaluation; when properly designed and conducted, they provide the most valid and reliable information obtainable with currently available technology about individuals perceptions of their needs, utilization patterns, and behavior.

The major disadvantages of this approach is its cost. In addition, some conditions (health, economic) are so variable in their definition that it is difficult to know when a condition is problematic. The very fine lines between states of health and states of illness are cases in point. A further problem is that many individuals are reluctant to provide some kinds of information, particularly in areas possibly considered illegal, immoral, embarrassing, or extremely private.

Warheit et al. [4] discuss needs assessment from the perspective of planning, and not all of the approaches they outline are particularly useful for evaluation. Siegel, Attkisson, and Cohn [11], writing from the perspective of evaluation, discuss three nonsurvey approaches to needs assessment, omitting rates under treatment and social indicators but adding the use or workshops—the nominal group approach [12]. Rates under treatment and social indicators do have some current or potential utility in program evaluation but not primarily in the area of needs assessment.

Process Evaluation.   What goes on within the program (the box in Fig. 5.1) is the concern of process evaluation. There is considerable debate about whether it is a legitimate concern of program evaluation (see Chapter 2), but those who feel that it is generally include program monitoring, client tracking, cost accounting, compliance, indicators of adequacy, and general "goal directedness" under the heading "process evaluation". Because of the considerable doubt about the legitimacy and efficacy of process evaluation *as a type of program evaluation,* each of the above areas is discussed only briefly and in general terms.

Program monitoring is one of the most common forms of process evaluation and is becoming increasingly prominent. It may involve nothing more than a cataloging of what services are offered and what are not, little more than a variant of effort evaluation or basic statistics. Usually, however, monitoring implies a kind of impressionistic comparative evaluation. Wholey et al., who consider program monitoring an "evaluation related" activity, define it:

> . . . the assessment of managerial and operational efficiency of programs or projects through periodic site visits and other management techniques. The usual objective of monitoring is to give program managers impressionistic data about how their projects are going, to see if they are being run efficiently, if they are following program guidelines, if they have competent staffs—in general, to do a management assessment of the soundness of individual projects. [13:27]

Wholey also maintains that program monitoring is not a legitimate activity for program evaluation and is, in reality, a focus on inputs. Nevertheless, much that goes on in the process of program monitoring does involve process evaluation, for example, patterns of referral, adequacy of reporting, service coordination, and others.

Client tracking, as the term suggests, is an attempt to monitor the progress of a client through a system. In its basic form it is part of a statistical system to report on the admission, transfer, movement, and exit of clients. With more elaboration, information concerning points of decision making, nature and type of communication about clients, referral patterns, and other such matters can be added. Sometimes programs have specified steps or procedures by which clients "should" progress through a program. If such steps or procedures exist the "actual" and the "ideal" progression of clients through a service system can be compared. The purpose of client tracking as a form of program evaluation is twofold. In large and complex social agencies and organizations, there is a danger that clients may "get lost" or "fall through the cracks," and client tracking is one way to minimize this danger.* When combined with service outcome, client tracking can provide valuable insights into the "client career" and with sufficient accumulated information can result in program orientations to direct clients into the best "track". Client tracking is also one approach to organizational analysis and can be useful for improving the efficiency and responsiveness of an organization's structure and processes.

A valuable form of process evaluation coming from business is cost accounting. Cost accounting is essential to the evaluation of program efficiency because it informs the

---

* In health oriented systems, this is frequently referred to as "continuity of care" but may also be used to assess the flow of clients from one to another type, locus, or intensity of treatment.

manager as to the cost of delivering different types of services. The danger is that, particularly on the part of funding sources, "cheapest" may be equated with "best," and efficiency may be confused with effectiveness. Cost accounting by itself cannot address the question of program effectiveness.

Most social programs have some requirements and prohibitions—certain legally defined limits within which the program may operate but beyond which the program is prohibited from operating. Unlike standards, discussed below, questions of compliance deal with requirements and prohibitions and are usually legislatively mandated rather than professionally developed. Typically, these requirements and prohibitions do not address program quality or program effectiveness but rather the safety and protection of program participants. Every major social program has a number of such requirements and restrictions relevant only to its sphere or operation, but examples that apply to most programs would include fire safety and sanitary regulations, child labor laws, minimum wage laws, fair employment practices laws, laws governing confidentiality or public access to information, civil rights, and so on. The inspection and monitoring for compliance in these areas are sometimes considered a form of process evaluations, but such information contributes to program evaluation only when combined with other orders of data.

There are a number of techniques used to gauge or estimate the adequacy of programs, but which are less impressionistic than most program monitoring. For many programs, sets of standards collectively define knowledgeable professionals' best estimates of the correlates of program quality. Often these standards are codified to the extent that they become the minimal requirements for licensure, accreditation, or some other mechanisms of formal recognition or approval. A large library is no guarantee that books will be read, and a Ph.D. is no guarantee of teaching excellence; however, in the opinion of noted educators a quality college or university is not possible without an adequate library and a highly trained scholarly faculty; therefore, libraries and earned degrees are two factors of importance in the accreditation of colleges and universities. This kind of comparative evaluation was discussed in Chapter 3. Even in the absence of written standards, it is sometimes possible to get an indication of program adequacy based on the judgments of experts—the appropriateness of an organization's structure to its function, the adequacy of staff size and composition, and the adequacy of accounting procedures are examples.

Another general indicator of adequacy is service accessibility. Problems of accessibility are usually related to the question of whether a program is serving all those it was designed to serve. The analysis of accessibility may involve questions of human ecology, public transportation, working hours, public visibility, and many others.

"Goal directedness" as an area of process evaluation refers not so much to the extent to which programs are achieving their goals as to the degree to which programs are actively pursuing stated goals and policies. For example, a generally accepted goal of community mental health centers is that they should develop and provide alternatives to state hospitalization. The extent to which a community program is actively and successfully pursuing such alternatives is a question for process evaluation.

Without reiterating the argument as to whether those

activities discussed above are proper and legitimate to the management subspecialty of program evaluation, two conclusions seem possible: With the possible exception of organizations analysis, process evaluation is the least developed and possibly the least important type of program evaluation; and if not evaluation activities, they are certainly evaluation related, and no program evaluation system can be complete without process information [13:27].

Outcome Evaluation. The assessment of program outcomes is the one area that everyone agrees is properly designated program evaluation, and a strong case can be made for the position that no activity should be labeled "evaluation" if it does not address results (see Chapter 2) [2, 13, 14, 15]. A number of techniques for outcome evaluation have already been discussed. Outcome evaluation addresses the question: "How have clients changed as a result of receiving services?" One of the most frequently utilized forms of outcome evaluation is the follow-up survey, which simply involves contacting a sample of clients who have received services to determine whether the problems or life situations that led the client to seek services have been substantially altered. Given the considerations of accuracy and economy, follow-up surveys are frequently the most satisfactory form of outcome evaluation. They have all of the weaknesses of the after-only designs discussed in Chapter 3 and are amenable to the refinements discussed in that chapter. By measuring at different points in time and the use of a control sample, such surveys more closely resemble before-after designs and quasi-experimental designs. They also become more costly [14]. As with any problem calling for surveys, the validity and reliability of the results and, therefore, the utility of the survey depend upon the care with which it is designed and conducted. Ultimately, the compromise between rigor and cost will be determined by the manager's need and the contraints on resources, including time.

Follow-up surveys, especially in the absence of controls, present the manager and evaluator with problems of interpretation. Because human service organizations tend to be structured around certain identified problem areas— health, mental health, education, welfare, disability, employment, and so on—and life experiences are *not* isolated and compartmentalized, follow-up studies are not able to establish direct causal linkages between the receipt of specific services and a subsequent life situation. The methodological problem was explained in Chapter 3.

The importance of establishing causal relationships varies. In some instances saying "these services were rendered, and clients are now functioning thus and so" is sufficient, and the question of causality is avoided altogether. Because usually no information at all exists about client outcome, any information can be of benefit to managers. A number of procedures have been used to limit the degree of uncertainty about the relationship of service activity to subsequent outcomes. One of the simplest is to ask the former client to evaluate the benefit or lack of benefit derived from services received—a measure of client satisfaction.

If properly used, client satisfaction is a valid form of program assessment but should not be used except in combination with other measures. In many respects the individual is the best living expert on his/her own life experiences. The problem is that there is a strong human tendency for the recipients of services to report satisfaction with these services—even when these "services" seemed to an outside observer to be blatantly punitive or when the deliverer of these services is disappointed with his efforts. Satisfaction percentages in the range of 60 to 80 percent are so common as to be considered the norm. Despite these difficulties, client satisfaction remains an important component of outcome evaluations, and practitioners may have higher expectations of their efforts than do their clients.

Another approach to reduce the uncertainty about the relationship of program activities to outcomes is that of goal attainment. There are several variant schemes of goal attainment (see bibliography and Chapter 3), but they have in common an attempt to limit outcome evaluation to the specific problems the client presents rather than to some more general concept of "adjustment" or "adequate functioning." Specifying the desired outcome lessens the problem of assigning causality. No practical method currently exists for eliminating all variables, other than the services received, which might influence the observed outcome. Goal attainment narrows the range of possible alternative explanations. The major problems are the expense of implementing and maintaining such methods and the fact that most human service professionals are not trained to think and practice in such terms.

Most human services programs and agencies offer some direct services to their consumers. Most, in addition, include as part of their mandates prevention activities and indirect services—often labeled as education and consultation. Prevention, as the word implies, is directed at the causes of the focal problem, not merely with alleviating the suffering of its victims. Indirect services include attempts to

utilize scarce professional expertise in assisting more numerous and available personnel to prevent the focal problem or to make early detection and thereby maximize the
possibility of successful intervention.

The problems of evaluating indirect services are particularly acute. Primarily, these problems center around the
definition of and, therefore, measurement of success. It is
difficult to know, for instance, how to measure the success
of an educational effort, especially if it is conducted outside
the traditional setting of the classroom. The success of
consultation, which is usually aimed either at giving advice
or at broadening the range of alternatives of the consultee,
are even more difficult. There is no obligation (stated or implied) on the part of the consultee to accept the advice or
to choose one of the newly offered alternatives. The satisfaction expressed by the recipients of such services is the
most commonly adopted criterion of success, but it places
the evaluation of such programs in the same category as
popularity contests [3:41]. To the extent that the goals for
education and consultation programs can be explicitly
specified, the problems of evaluation are lessened and can
utilize the techniques outlined in the previous chapters.
The problems of evaluating prevention activities—or what
would have happened if some activity had not occurred—
defy present evaluation technologies. The closest approxi-
mation is in the use of social indicators and trend data (discussed below), but these are only approximations.

The area of indirect services is one in which the
technology of evaluation does not exceed the technology
of program providers, a charge that has been leveled in
regard to direct services. The development of methodologies for the assessment of indirect services remains

one of the most pressing needs in the area of program evaluation.

By far the most promising area for outcome evaluation combines the concerns of business management and human services accountability; it is cost-benefit analysis. Cost-benefit analysis combines cost analysis, including the monitoring of patient movement and the identification of where and how costs are incurred, with an analysis of the benefits received by the clients served. Unfortunately, the technology for cost-benefit analysis in human services is not well developed. The problem is in defining and isolating a unit of benefit—a problem that is both conceptual and methodological. Costs can be analyzed and units of service defined (usually in terms of the expenditure of staff time); but what constitutes an increment of benefit has only rarely been successfully scaled. Benefit in a gross sense can sometimes be ascertained, but what constitutes one unit, or three units, or whatever, cannot be ascertained—much less whether 10 units is twice the improvement of five units. The work of Binner [16, 17] and his associates on output-value analysis is an interesting and important beginning in the development of thorough cost-benefit analysis, a vitally important area in which considerable development is needed.

Impact Evaluation. Most major social programs are intended to alleviate some identified problems known to be widespread in a population. In the case of public programs, there is a decision on the part of public policymakers that the alleviation of the condition is a public responsibility and the receipt of services for individuals who need them is a citizen's right, not a privilege. Free public education is a prototype of this model. Major social legislation has been intended to have an impact, not only on the individual recipients of the services provided, but also upon communities and the citizenry as a whole. The determination of that impact is enormously difficult, in part because of the already mentioned confounding of factors. One of the most promising but as yet largely unrealized areas of impact evaluation is the development of social indicators.

Social indicators were discussed briefly as a technique for needs assessment. From the perspective of evaluation, the major purpose of the assessment of need is the assessment of impact. For this reason, the social indicators most commonly used as indirect measures of need cannot be used for the evaluation of program impact. For example, high rates of crime, unemployment, and divorce have been used (with some justification) as indicators of the need for mental health services. However, no one has been naive enough to suggest that a reduction in crime, increasing employment, and less divorce attest to the efficacy of mental health programs. In the area of economics, indicators have been highly successful in aiding administrators in setting policy and in judging the success of these policies. Such indicators as the Gross National Product, new housing starts, and others have proved to be quite sensitive in monitoring the state of the economy. In areas other than economics, and to a certain extent education, sensitive social indicators have been elusive, but the situation is far from bleak. The success and history of economic indicators has been somewhat blinding; people tend to forget that in the 1930s, when most of the economic indicators were developed, enormous effort and mental anguish went into their development. The ready availability of data was cited as an advantage in using social indicators for planning. For decision making and evaluation, however, quite the opposite conclusion was reached by a "blue-ribbon" presidential panel, appointed in 1966, as they stated the problem:

> Only a small fraction of the existing statistics tell us anything about social conditions, and those that do often point in different directions. Sometimes they do not add up to any meaningful conclusion and they are not very useful to either the policy maker or the concerned citizen. The government normally does not publish statistics on whether or not children are learning more than they used to, or on whether social mobility is increasing or decreasing. It does publish statistics on life expectancy and the incidence of disability due to ill health, but some diseases are becoming more common and others less common, and no summary measure indicating whether we could expect more healthy life has been available. [18:96]

The report goes on to point out that the lack of adequate statistics is not the result of lack of effort; it refers to a report issued in 1967 which noted that the federal government employed 18,902 statistical workers and spent $88 million on automatic data processing, computer equipment, and statistical studies under contract with private firms. The report concludes that a reassessment of what statistics should be collected is needed.

There have, of course, been many subsequent attempts to arrive at meaningful social indicators, most recently a number of "quality of life" scales have been developed, but these too have been greeted with minimal enthusiasm [19].

The difficulty of developing meaningful social indicators with reasonable consensus about what they indicate is multiplied many times over when they are applied to smaller geographic units and to a single area of social activity, such as health, education, criminal justice, and so on. Perhaps, as has been suggested, social indicators are not a realistic tool for the evaluation of a program.

A frequently expressed objective of community programs is that they impact not simply on direct or indirect consumers of services, but also on the social ecology of the entire community. Probably, neither our knowledge nor our current programs match the loftiness of this goal. It has become clear over the past decade that achievement of the community impact goal is not the prerogative of any one type of human service agency. Instead, planning, coordination and exchange of information are required among the whole array of human services within communities. The participation of citizens is also a necessary, if sometimes problematic, contribution to the decision-making process. Without these two ingredients— the cooperation of service agencies and citizen participation—it is unreasonable to expect any single service program to have a tangible impact on the total community. [20:44]

Nevertheless, program evaluation is one of the major thrusts in the current search for social indicators, and despite the present state of the art, they should not be easily dismissed.

Good decisions must be based on a careful evaluation of the facts. This truism is so often the basis for our most mundane behavior that we are seldom aware of its far-reaching significance. Most people do not decide whether to carry an umbrella without first checking the weather forecast or at least glancing out the window to see if it is raining. Yet, those policymakers and citizens who are concerned about the condition of American society often lack the information they need in order to decide what, if anything, should be done about the state of that society. Without the right kind of facts, they are not able to discern emerging problems, or to make informed decisions about national priorities. Nor are they able to choose confidently between alternative solutions to these problems or decide how much money should be allocated to any given program. [18:95]

A second approach to the analysis of program impact relates back to the survey approach to the assessment of need—the actual change in the level of need from one point in time to another. This involves periodic resurveying a population, and with the exception of the decennial census, few organizations have expended the necessary resources for such admittedly expensive activities (see discussion of pretest-posttest designs).

In this section we have discussed evaluation in terms of a simplified systems model and indicated that there are evaluation questions of importance to managerial decision making at each point in the system. In addition, there is a temporal logic in the typology moving from the identification of need, through the analysis of services to the identification of impact. Figure 5.2 graphically summarizes these types of evaluation, incorporating a time dimension into the basic systems diagram.

EVALUATION AS A MANAGEMENT FUNCTION. Evaluation is a series of discrete activities directed at specific results. In addition, evaluation is a function of management and must be related to, and integrated with, other management functions. Managerial functions have been categorized in a number of ways, but this discussion uses a very common threefold categorization—planning, implementation, and control. Although they are related, they are

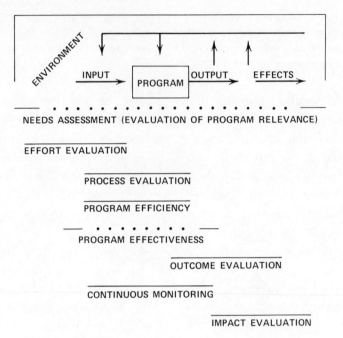

Figure 5.2.   A systems/process evaluation typology.

considered separately because the relevance of evaluation to each is somewhat different.

Planning.   An a managerial function, planning involves the declaration of intent and a determination among available alternatives for implementation. Planning in social programs is usually a response to perceived or demonstrated shortcomings, unmet needs, or the requirements of legislation. It is not a particularly popular activity and, like evaluation, is viewed by some as a diversion of resources and energies from the primary activity of service delivery. A number of formal planning methodologies do exist (see Chapter 3) which accommodate the fact that programs, once planned, must be evaluated, but their use remains more the exception than the rule. Most of these methodologies were developed in business, industry, or the military and have had to be substantially modified for social programs. While formal planning methodologies have not been the boon to social program managers it was hoped they would, their use has been beneficial in that they have motivated the development of planning methodologies better suited to the needs of social programs.

What formal planning methodologies have in common is the specification of the desired outcome prior to the inception of a program or, for an ongoing program, within a specified time. This process is a clear and laudable response to the fact, mentioned in the *Introduction*, that the mere provision of services is no longer sufficient justification for their continuation. Because such planning involves the specification of desired outcomes or anticipated levels of activity, it specifies the focus of future evaluations and shares many problems with evaluation activities.

The adoption of formal planning methodologies brings with it special problems for managers and their staff specialists and places them in an unaccustomed, and often uncomfortable, position. In the first place, the "goals," or "objectives," or whatever they are called, must be realistic. Because managers must usually operate without any firm knowledge of what their programs are accomplishing or what portion of the population in need they are currently reaching, realistic expectations are almost impossible to determine. Goals and objectives must also be measurable, and this imposes another set of problems. Most managers are unaccustomed to thinking in terms of measurement and are not acquainted with the sources of data available, the record keeping needed to collect such information, nor what is involved in measurement. The result is often goals which seem designed purely for the frustration of the evaluator. The evaluator should be involved in the planning process, particularly in the specification of measurements because this is the point in the planning-implementation-evaluation cycle at which major responsibility shifts. In fact, the major role of the evaluator in the planning process should be to ensure that the structure and process of planning is such that evaluation is possible.

One example should suffice. Goals or objectives such as "to reduce by 25 percent the incidence of drug abuse" often appear early in a program planning effort. Such goals are symptomatic of managers' tendencies to overlook certain facts: (1) There is no easy or even effective way to determine the level of drug abuse, much less measure its reduction; (2) the assessment of the level of drug abuse may be more expensive than the program aimed at its reduction; (3) the success of other programs (such as law enforcement) may be more important to the reduction of drug abuse than the proposed program; and (4) as stated, the goal does not, and cannot, determine that the proposed program is more effective than current programs or no program at all.

From the perspective of program evaluation, one of the most conceptually elegant of the formal planning methodologies is Key Factor Analysis, which incorporates the systems and goal attainment models, discussed in Chapter 4, and the social indicator approach to impact, discussed above. Its elegance stems from the fact that it requires managers to specify the intended impact of an organization (in terms of population characteristics) *independently* of the goals of existing or planned activities (such goals often expressed in terms of client or organizational characteristics) [21]. Despite its logical consistency and conceptual elegance, at the time of this writing, no organization has been able to implement Key Factor Analysis fully, and the reasons are instructive for program evaluation. Although analysis of problems continues, we can conclude that among the reasons Key Factor Analysis has never been implemented fully are: (1) it is heavily dependent upon an approach (social indicator analysis) of which the technology and substance are only slowly being developed; and (2) no organization has had the ability, or even the inclination, to commit the resources necessary to develop and maintain the enormous data base and information system required by Key Factor Analysis.

Both problems are relevant to program evaluation and may occur to some degree with the use of any formal planning methodology that includes an evaluation component. The lesson to be learned is that the manager and the evaluator, in the planning of new, expanded, or continued programs must be certain that the desired results are specified and that there are adequate technologies and sufficient resources to determine whether or to what degree those accomplishments have been realized.

What this rather extended discussion is intended to show is that planning and evaluation are intrinsically linked as different arcs in the same circle. Planning, in the absence of meaningful evaluation, is largely an empty exercise, but in fact, systematic planning is rare and the evaluator is often left with salvaging what he can. Some organizations have adopted formal planning methodologies in response to this problem (and other problems, beyond the scope of this book), but the evaluation demands created by the utilization of these methodologies may be beyond the abilities of current technology or available resources. Planning and evaluation, as management functions, must proceed concurrently.

Implementation (Organizing, Staffing, Directing).   Once a decision is made to initiate or continue a program, the problems and roles of the evaluator change. Implementation is the function of management that least involves the evaluator. The concern of managers at this point is with the "nitty-gritty"—the location and allocation of resources, the coordination with other programs, "selling" the program to potential users or backers, coping with problems of personnel morale that may accompany any major change in direction or introduction of new activities. Program implementation and program evaluation are linked only to the extent that evaluation provides information to managers on program operation, outcome, and so on; but in certain situations implementation and evaluation must be integrated and pursued concurrently. This integration is necessary, for example, when established standards exist and managers need answers to the questions: Does the program meet requirements for such programs? Is implementation proceeding on schedule? How does this program compare with others similar in nature (comparative evaluation)? In short, if the systems model is considered legitimate or if process evaluation is important, evaluation and implementation become somewhat interwoven.

Another situation in which evaluation and implementation come into congruence is in the area of client tracking, discussed earlier in the chapter. Other types of evaluation involve both the implementation and control functions and are discussed in the next section.

Control. Control is the single management function in which evaluation is ascendant. In fact, some managers, who dislike the connotation of the term *control* mistakenly label all such activities "evaluation." Control is management's ultimate reason for making use of program evaluation. The use of information to make, or to decide against, changes in programs is the essential control function of management and the desired utilization of evaluation. But, while evaluation—not necessarily program evaluation (see Chapter 2)—is the basis of all control *functions,* program evaluation itself is not the proper basis for all control *decisions.* For instance, personnel changes may be one result of program evaluation, but more likely they would result from broader kinds of evaluation of performance and ability, the aftermath of administrative changes, or most frequently, routine staffing decisions that are a part of the implementation function, not part of the control function.

The allocation of resources is one area in which the use of program evaluation to inform is quite appropriate. All social programs pursue multiple goals and do so with limited resources. Decisions about how to allocate these resources should involve a judgment about how to maximize effectiveness. The more information formal evaluation can contribute for these decisions, the more these decisions are likely to be rational. Some of the contributions of program evaluation to the control function of management (including resource allocation) are listed below in the form of questions concerning human service programs that evaluation can assist in answering. All of these have been discussed elsewhere.

1.   Where should resources be directed?

These decisions could result from the assessment of need—for example, the determination of underserved populations—or from a determination of program effectiveness. Program evaluation may also be useful in decisions to direct resources away from one program element and into another, although such applications of program evaluation remain rare.

2.   Which among alternative ways of accomplishing similar goals should be supported?

This is comparative evaluation in its purest form and involves both process and outcome evaluation. A variant of this use of evaluation would be a decision to implement, on a system-wide basis, a successful program that had been initiated on an experimental or demonstration basis.

3.   How should resources, particularly manpower resources, be organized?

As stated, this question belongs equally in the realms of implementation and control but is discussed here because some of the subquestions it involves get to issues of program continuation, which is the most basic of all controlling decisions. The initial question gets at the heart of program effectiveness, and with the addition of financial resources, efficiency. Just a few of the possible decisions are noted here.

a. How can resource allocation be properly balanced between the delivery of services and the administration of these services? Clearly, the extreme options are absurd. Administration in the absence of services is the ultimate in bureaucratic boondoggling. Services in the absence of administration results in chaos—duplication, lack of coordination, improper staffing, inadequate communication, confusion of responsibility and accountability, territoriality, and so on. The loser in each of these extremes is the client. The distance between the extremes is enormous, and the balance between them a constant source of contention and negotiation. The basic question is how to optimize results— essentially an evaluation question, but curiously program evaluation is particularly vulnerable. Some managers and practitioners argue that any expenditure of funds for evaluation diverts funds and efforts from direct services and is therefore unjustified. Others maintain that evaluation is necessary for the protection of the client, the justification of program continuation, and all the other functions discussed in this volume. Other administrative functions are not subject to this type of questioning; the fact that evaluation is singled out in this respect is a reflection of the history and issues outlined in the *Introduction*, elaborated in Chapter 4.

b. Given an allocation of resources, how should they be configured? This is the basic question of organizational structure, involving matters such as span of control, delineation and delegation of authority, lines of responsibility, the impact of ideology and the appropriate exercise of power. The evaluator can be of considerable value in these matters, particularly by indicating strengths and weaknesses of current or proposed arrangements, different outcomes of different arrangements, and so on. Again, such activities are a combination of implementation and control; for the evaluator, they should be addressed from the position of maximizing results.

c. At what point should resources be withheld from a program? This, of course, is the ultimate sanction and one exercised with great reluctance. It is often the one most easily and most often subject to purely political manipulation. Assuming a degree of rationality, the most frequent way such decisions are made involves the application of minimal acceptable standards or assessments concerning compliance with legal requirements. Ideally, these decisions are based on information gained through program evaluation, although rarely evaluation of the research variety. The role of the evaluator is to assure, by whatever appropriate means, that strengths and shortcomings are fully and accurately documented and that such documentation is in terms of the intended and achieved results of the program. This particular use of evaluation is seldom invoked for two reasons: Most social programs are operated on personalistic rather than universalistic criteria [22], and many decisions are politically motivated and may reflect considerable lack of consensus among political subunits. The most successful application of this type of control, and thus evaluation, comes in instances in which a designated official or agency has a clear public mandate to stop the activity completely—violation of fire safety standards, sanitation regulations, electrical wiring ordinances, or anything that involves licensure. Most often considerations of the withholding or withdrawal of resources flounder on questions of "adequacy" (a matter of opinion) or "effectiveness" (about which there is rarely information.). For whatever reason, the vagaries of applying this type of program control have given rise to the often voiced question and criticism: "How many programs have been terminated as a result of evaluation?" The question is a fair one, and the best answer is: "Very few." However, such questioning is usually used to illustrate the ineffectual role of evaluation and almost never recognizes the fact that decisions to use or refrain from using evaluation are independent of the evaluation effort. Too often, the decision not to utilize evaluation information is assumed a *priori* to reflect upon the quality of the evaluation rather than the skills and responsibilities of the manager.

Many other kinds of managerial control decisions involve evaluation; ideally, most of them do. These are only illustrative. This volume is devoted to explaining what evaluation is and how it is done. Problems and opportunities are a part of that concern. Ideally, evaluation is linked to all management functions but is of particular relevance, although not of notable application, in the area of control.

SUMMARY. Figure 5.3 illustrates in a simplistic manner the interrelationships among the functions of management. The box represents management and the circles represents the functions of management. While there are areas of overlap (and these have been discussed above), there are also areas of independent concern. The relationship of research to both evaluation and management is discussed later, but it does indicate that *some* evaluation is research,

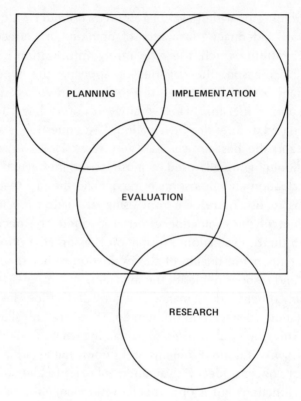

Figure 5.3.   The interrelated functions of management.

as was indicated earlier, but most research is not evaluation.

Because program evaluation overlaps with the other functions of management and with other specialties, a real problem for managers is where to place program evaluators in the management structure. The internal-external dilemma was discussed earlier. Usually, evaluation is a small and limited endeavor, especially at its initiation, and the manager usually has demands upon his attention so great as to constitute sensory overload. When the evaluator enters the scene, therefore, the natural tendency of the administrator is to combine evaluation with, or append it to, an already existing administrative subunit with a related or overlapping activity. Organizational subunits entitled "Planning and Evaluation," "Standards and Evaluation," "Research and Evaluation," "Statistics and Evaluation" are common. In part, these combinations reflect organizational history; in part, disciplinary interests. For instance, although the Comprehensive Community Mental Health Centers Act (1963) requires evaluation (one of the requirements not enforced), program evaluation is not mentioned as one of the "essential services" but is instead listed, in combination with research, as one of the "adequate services." The fact that in a major piece of legislation it is at once required and not required is a reflection of a general confusion about what program evaluation actually encompasses. We will return to this point shortly, but it may be clarified somewhat now by examining the fate of evaluation in combination with related activities. As might be expected, evaluation has historically fared badly in these combined subunits.

The most common combination of activities is that of planning and evaluation. Planning has preceded evaluation both in historical emergence and in the management cycle. Planning emerged as a management subspecialty before evaluation and is therefore better established, and in a temporal sequence of planning, implementation, and evaluation, planning precedes evaluation. The result usually is that, when planning and evaluation are combined in a single organizational subunit, most of the resources and energy go into planning. There is evidence that this imbalance is being redressed as evaluation "comes of age" and as managers of social programs become increasingly sophisticated in the coordination of management functions.

A combination of activities of more recent emergence is

that of standards and evaluation. This, also, seems a logical combination. One of the increasingly prominent types of process evaluation is the comparison of program performance against established standards. In addition, many federal block grants require the establishment of standards as a condition of funding. The intent of these requirements is quality control and evaluation. However, evaluation again is often seriously diluted. In the establishment of standards, many states require public hearings prior to their adoption, and this procedure is enormously time consuming. Public hearings are for the benefit and protection of the public and are therefore crucially important. However, the legal requirements around standards frequently mean that concerns for evaluation are postponed because evaluation is neither protected nor encumbered by the same legal requirements. More importantly, the highly structured and relatively comfortable focus upon compliance to standards can easily result in the more crucial but more difficult question—the relationship of standards of care to the outcomes of care—being ignored. There is then a great deal of activity in the name of evaluation without the central questions of evaluation ever being addressed.

The combination of evaluation and research is considerably more complicated. Many evaluators come to their task from research backgrounds (usually social and behavioral research) and see their activities in the high status context of research. More importantly, program evaluation does utilize the techniques of research; in fact, most of the best evaluation is research. The problem arises because *research* is a generic term encompassing a multitude of intents, and *program evaluation* is a generic term that only sometimes encompasses research in its most scientific connotations. The important distinctions here are the definitions of research: Is it a universal process in rational problem solving or is it a specialized technique available only to the initiated? In truth, it is both. It is a highly disciplined method for arriving at the best informed conclusions through logical, sequential, ordered thinking; and it is a method that requires specialized training. The problem for evaluation arises when research is equated with a rigorous experimental method (one type of research). Referring back to Figure 5.3, the major portion of the circle representing research is outside the square representing management. This is not meant to imply that most research is conducted outside the boundaries of an organization— quite the opposite is true. What Figure 5.3 is intended to portray is that the bulk of research activity is basic research and as such must be freed from the immediate constraints and demands of management. The management problem is to ensure that basic research has the necessary freedom to pursue the quest for new knowledge. For evaluation, an organizational combination with research presents some special problems, here simply enumerated.

1. The rigors of the experimental method can only rarely be approached by program evaluation, thus making it incomparable to basic research and subject to inappropriate criticisms.

2. Basic research was never intended to be immediately applicable to social programs. As a result, the identification of evaluation with research offers the reluctant manager an excuse to overlook evaluation findings and, in some instances, to excuse himself from his responsibility for evaluation.

3. In the course of the past two decades, enormous safeguards have been built, rightfully, to protect experimental subjects—both human and other animals. The subject of evaluation is the program, not the person, and to subject a nonexperimental management function to the procedures designed for experimental subjects negates much of the potential usefulness of program evaluation for the requirements of the manager. Safeguards, more relevant to program evaluation, must be developed.

In this chapter we have attempted to outline, from a variety of perspectives, the relationship of program evaluation to the functions of management. We have examined some of the special problems of program evaluation and have concluded, by implication, that program evaluation should be closely identified with top management and as free from competitive identifications as is organizationally and programmatically feasible.

REFERENCES

1. L. Mitchell, "An Interview Study Points Out The Problem With 'Contract' Evaluations," *Evaluation,* I, 21–23 (#2, 1973).
2. Edward Suchman, *Evaluative Research,* Russell Sage Foundation, New York, 1967.
3. Carol Weiss, *Evaluation Research,* Prentice-Hall, Englewood Cliffs, N.J., 1972.
4. George J. Warheit, Roger A. Bell, and John J. Schwab, *Planning for Change: Needs Assessment Approaches,* National Institute of Mental Health, Washington, D.C., no date.
5. R. E. L. Farris and H. W. Dunham, *Mental Disorders in Urban Areas,* University of Chicago Press, Chicago, 1939.
6. A. B. Hollingshead and F. C. Redlich, *Social Class and Mental Illness: A Community Study,* Wiley, New York, 1958.
7. Eshref Shevsky and Marilyn Williams, *The Social Areas of Los Angeles,* University of California Press, Berkeley, 1949.

8. Eshref Shevsky and Wendell Bell, *Social Area Analysis,* Stanford University Press, Palo Alto, 1955.

9. W. S. Robinson, "Ecological Correlation and the Behavior of Individuals," *American Sociological Review,* XV, 351–357 (June 1950).

10. John L. Hammond, "Two Sources of Error in Ecological Correlations," *American Sociological Review,* XXXVIII, 764–777 (December 1973).

11. Larry Siegel, C. Clifford Attkisson, and Anne Cohn, "Mental Health Needs Assessment: Strategies and Techniques," in William Hargreaves et al. (eds.), *Resource Material for Community Mental Health Program Evaluation: Part II Needs Assessment and Planning,* National Institute of Mental Health, Washington, D.C., 1974.

12. A. L. Delberg and A. H. Van De Ven, "A Group Process Model for Problem Identification and Program Planning," *Journal of Applied Behavioral Science,* IV, 466–492 (1971).

13. Joseph S. Wholey et al., *Federal Evaluation Policy,* The Urban Institute, Washington, D.C., 1970.

14. James Ciarlo, "A Performance-Monitoring Approach to Mental Health Program Evaluation," (January 1972) mimeo.

15. Herbert Schulberg, Alan Sheldon and Frank Baker (eds.), *Program Evaluation in the Health Fields,* Behavioral Publications, New York, 1969.

16. Paul R. Binner and Joseph Halpern, "Output Value Analysis: A Model for the Evaluation of Mental Health Programs," *Program Evaluation Forum Position Papers,* Program Evaluation Project, Minneapolis, 1971.

17. Paul Binner, "Program Evaluation," in Saul Feldman (ed.), *The Administration of Mental Health Services,* Charles C. Thomas, Springfield, Ill., 1973, pp. 342–383.

18. President's Panel on Social Indicators, *Toward A Social Report,* U.S. Government Printing Office, Washington, D.C., 1969.

19. Leslie Wilcox et al., *Social Indicators and Societal Monitoring,* Josey Bass, San Francisco, 1972.

20. C. Clifford Attkisson et al., *A Working People's Guide to Community Mental Health Program Evaluation Literature,* The Program Evaluation Project, Department of Psychiatry, University of California, San Francisco, 1973.

21. *Key Factor Analysis Workbook,* Raleigh, N.C., Jarett, Rader and Longhurst, 1970.

22. Talcott Parsons, *The Social System,* Free Press, Glencoe, Ill., 1951.

6
Quo Vadis?

The preceding chapters have been designed to accomplish three tasks.

1. To outline the field of program evaluation, indicating the sources and emergence of program evaluation as a management subspecialty. The parameters of program evaluation were delineated and the present state-of-the-art described. This description shows that program evaluation as a formal activity is a recent addition to the manager's armamentarium and is still very much an emergent institutional activity.

2. To present and discuss some of the more common models and methods used in the actual evaluation of social programs. The discussion centered on the methodologies and techniques an evaluator can use in his work, as well as

some of the compromises and trade-offs that may be necessary. This part of the presentation was intended as a "how-to-do-it" and "what-to-look-out-for" discussion.

3. To examine evaluation within the context of management functions and the system of management decisions. The focus continued to be upon evaluation and the role and possible tasks of the evaluator, but from the perspective of organizational requirements and programmatic decisions.

Throughout the earlier chapters the point was stressed repeatedly that the characteristic that distinguishes program evaluation from other information-gathering activities and other review and monitoring activities (as well as management control functions generally) is the focus upon program outcomes. Other activities may or may not be part of evaluation, depending upon how they were used, but as a matter of organizational accommodation evaluators may need to engage in activities that are only indirectly related to the central evaluation task.

This chapter includes some extrapolation of trends and some outright prognostication to attempt to review and suggest some future directions and developments for program evaluation and some of the ways that current dilemmas may be resolved. The short-term future tasks for evaluation as a field of endeavor are threefold: identification, consolidation, routinization. Although this chapter concentrates largely on the latter, no step can be omitted in the development of evaluation in any organization. Therefore, the first two problems are discussed briefly.

In Chapters 2 and 4 we devoted considerable attention to the identity problems of program evaluation as an emerging subspecialty. The primary sources of the development and identification were an increasingly urgent calling for the public accountability of public programs, and service institutions had "begun to realize that, at present, they are not being managed" [1:45]. Against this formidable thrust were equally formidable resistances, not the least of which was the inertia of institutional history. More important for the development of program evaluation, however, were the resistances from administrators with little knowledge or interest in management, the threatening nature of evaluation, managers' greater reliance on hunches than upon data, occupational territoriality, and the dilution of the thrust and intent of program evaluation to secure resources for the pursuit of private career interests [2, 3, 4, 5]. For these and the other reasons enumerated in the previous chapters, program evaluation in any organization must first be identified and legitimated as a formal activity different from other management activities and specialties congruent with them. Such a step requires the strong and active support of top management; but unless such a step is taken, both history and experience indicate that the central role and function will be diluted and subverted, although activities called evaluation may be ongoing.

Once program evaluation has been firmly identified and defined, it can be consolidated into the general structure of management. The forms this can take have been described in Chapters 2 and 5. How central a role program evaluation will play depends in large measure upon the organizational level of the activity and the pattern of centralization and decentralization in the structure of the organization. The higher one goes in the management structure, the more time a manager should spend on controlling activities, including evaluation. Therefore, at the top levels of management, evaluation by a specialized evaluation staff should be quite central to the management process. Patterns of decentralization and authority also influence the nature of evaluation consolidation. For instance, a common organizational pattern for public instructional programs in this country is to have highly autonomous local school systems responsible to locally elected boards yet accountable to a state authority for the quality and effectiveness of their programs. In this situation large and active evaluation units at the central (or state) level are common. As a generalization, we can say that the more decentralized an organization is, the greater the concern with evaluation at the top level. Whatever the final configuration, after evaluation has been formally identified and established and before it can be routinized, "role clarification," in which evaluation activities become consolidated and integrated in the management structure, is a necessary step.

THE ROUTINIZATION OF EVALUATION. After formal program evaluation has been initiated and developed, an organization can routinize some evaluation activities and information feedback, thus making it more efficient and timely. In fact, very few organizations have reached this enviable state, so the directions and expected benefits are largely inferential. One method of routinization, the propositional inventory, is briefly presented here, and the remainder of the chapter is devoted to a discussion of a very promising, but still undemonstrated, method of continuous monitoring, the automated management information system (MIS).

Propositional Inventories.   Glaser [6] suggests that a fruitful way to make program evaluation more routine and to guide efforts at discovery of new information is the development of propositional inventories. These are statements about known or strongly suspected relationships associated with various evaluation criteria, together with statements of the available evidence, evidence needed for confirmation and current levels of accomplishment (if they exist). Glaser gives the following example:

> Proposition:
>   The proportion of releasees returned to prison tends to be higher:
> a.   where probation is used extensively, so that only the worst risks go to prison (although this may make long-run recidivism rates of all felons lower);
> b.   where parole is used extensively, so that many poor risk parolees are released on a trial basis;
> c.   where a large proportion of parolees are returned to prison when they have violated parole regulations but have not been charged with or convicted of new felonies;
> d.   where there is a high overall crime rate in the communities to which prisoners are released, so that there is high prospect of the releasee coming from and going to highly criminogenic circumstances. [6:178]

Glaser goes on to note the inferences and evidence on which the proposition is based and what would be needed for conclusive documentation. Such propositional statements can be as general or as specific as managers need or available evidence permits. In suggesting propositional inventories as a solution to many of the complaints of evaluators and about evaluation, Glaser concludes:

> Evaluations too often are formulated in noncomparable terms, are reported in widely scattered publications, and con-

sequently provide only disconnected bits of knowledge that are noncumulative. This problem has not been diminished much by compiling huge collections of abstracts or appointing committees to draft manuals of standards, as by publishing highly selected abstracts and periodic articles summarizing knowledge and theory on specific topics. An even greater cumulative benefit could result from the periodic compilation of carefully edited inventories of propositions on people-changing issues, each followed by a summary of the theory and research relevant to it. If we routinized evaluative research and address it to testing items in the propositional inventory, yet do not make it so routine and so restricted to the inventory's items as to rule out imaginative new ideas and experiments, we shall maximize the effectiveness of people-changing endeavors. [6:182]

Management Information Systems (MIS). Another approach to the routinization of evaluation, one that is vastly different from propositional inventories, but is not mutually exclusive, is found in the resurgence of interest in automated information systems for social and human service agencies. Because of the great promise of these systems and because of their increasing prominence, the MIS approach to evaluation is discussed in some detail, including the rationale and incentives. The federal government, particularly the various National Institutes of Health, has recently been actively encouraging states to develop continuous monitoring systems which incorporate evaluation, and many states have responded with vigorous and imaginative efforts.

Ideally, evaluation is a necessary part of the human decision-making and learning processes. A model of rational decision making holds that an individual continually processes information, identifies the problem to be solved, solves the problem, evaluates the solution and adapts to and learns from the solution. The rational model maintains this process is so routinized that individuals rarely separate the process into discrete stages. Like any model, this is an heuristic device; probably few individual decisions are made so rationally.

The value of such a rational model of decision making is that it provides a convenient parallel between individual and organizational decision making, and from there to data-based management support systems. The primary difference between rational individual decision making and rational organizational decision making is that in the latter the steps are more discrete and more formal. In large organizations, specialized organizational subunits have developed that have as a major responsibility the assurance that the necessary input is available at each stage of the decision-making process. For instance, subunits of statistics, accounting, and so on routinely collect or process data on the state and status of the organization, in much the same way as temperature, pulse rate, and blood pressure are considered vital indicators of the general condition of an individual. Problems, often identified as exceptions to norms or expectations, are reported to managers, either by these or by other subunits.* Solutions to these problems may be suggested in various ways: specialized subunits, teams of senior staff who condense the available information and consider the problem and possible consequences from various viewpoints, consultant or resident specialists, and others. From the

---

* Clearly, problems identified in this way are those routinely expected or commonly encountered. Other orders of problems may be identified by anyone, anywhere in the organization. To continue the earlier analogy, a thermometer measures body temperature, but it is not particularly useful in diagnosing a learning disability. However, there are many more febrile disorders than there are learning disabilities.

available alternatives, a decision on a solution is reached; once determined, the efficacy of that solution is evaluated by whatever structure or structures have been developed for that purpose. The results of this process become a part of the organizational history and the personal and professional experiences of the participants. This process is diagrammatically summarized in Figure 6.1. In reality, many organizational decisions are not this rationally derived—a fact that provides one impetus for the development of automated information systems. Also in point of fact, the activities of data-and-information-producing subunits tend to overlap, although each subunit has a specific area of expertise.

Using Figure 6.1 as a generic model and building upon the advantages of routinizing program evaluation, in the following sections of this chapter we discuss two additional problems that could be ameliorated by routinization, how an automated MIS could be designed to alleviate these and other problems, some remaining uncertainties about an MIS as an evaluation mechanism, and some of the reasons why the potential of management information systems make their development well worth the risk and investment.

TWO PROBLEMS

Skilled Evaluation: Supply and Demand. In the past several years the demand for skilled evaluators has far exceeded the supply of in-house professionals and first-rate academic researchers willing to respond. Wholey notes that managers at the operating program level seldom are able to attract talented evaluators, even when positions and funds are available.

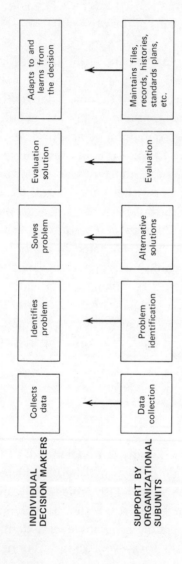

Figure 6.1. A model of rational decision-making.

The Office of Education Bureau of Elementary and Secondary Education, for example, has had a recruiting problem ever since it was established. OEO program officers said they were not handicapped by lack of evaluation funds but by a critical shortage of in-house staff to use these funds efficiently. Part of the recruiting problem results from the poor image that university professors and students have of federal program evaluation. [7:83]

The shortage of in-house talent and the lack of interested academic personnel encourage the use of contracted evaluation. However, the lack of in-house talent to assess adequately the program's evaluation needs, to supervise the contractors, and to transmit the results back to decision makers tends to decrease the effectiveness of contract evaluation (see Chapter 5).

Lynn suggests that a federal evaluation bureau is needed, but he also points out the supply-demand discrepancy.

To help meet the need, nonprofit research organizations and profit-making management consulting firms have increased in number and size and in the extent to which they seek to do policy-relevant analyses and evaluations. Some of their work has been excellent, but most of it has been disappointing. Part of the problem is that too few really first-rate researchers and evaluators are associated with these organizations. [8:57]

Lynn further notes the lack of skilled in-house officials who have the skills, time and power to guide and direct these contractors [8].

One unfortunate accommodation to the lack of qualified evaluators has been that responsibilities for the conduct and supervision of evaluation activities are added to the responsibilities of officials who have other tasks (see

Chapter 5). The result is that evaluation activities are assigned rather low priorities and frequently are conducted by persons with little training in evaluation methodology. A recent survey of federally funded mental health facilities (which have a strong mandate to evaluate their performances) indicated that of the facilities that responded, a little over a third (37.8 percent) have full-time evaluators, but a little under a third (29.8 percent) had no one with that designated responsibility. In addition, of those programs that had full- or part-time evaluators, nearly a third (32.1 percent) either had no collegiate degree or the degree was unknown, even though the skills most frequently identified as essential to the tasks (evaluation, probability and statistics, experimental design/methodology, management or administrative systems/techniques) are not those likely to be acquired casually in a baccalaureate curriculum or even in advanced clinically oriented training [9].

The need for training programs, at the collegiate level, for program evaluators is acute. The extent of the need is so great that fairly immediate adaptations must be made in the management of programs so that available expertise can be most efficiently and effectively utilized—that is, the routinizing of the routinizable. How an integrated MIS may be one response to this dilemma is discussed later.

The Use of Scientific Information.   The lack of skills and proper orientation for the effective use of evaluative information appears to be widespread among managers. A study of the use of scientific information reveals that officials are eager to obtain objective information but often do not know how to use such information in decision making.* Caplan identified three basic cognitive orientations which characterize managers' use of scientific information and its importance in decision making.

The Clinical Orientation. Managers in this category are considered the most effective users of scientific information. They are able to amass and analyze the best available objective information on any issue under consideration and to make decisions relatively free of personal bias—what Caplan calls the internal logic of problem solving. However, managers with this orientation are cognizant of social and political constraints—the external logic—which also influence their decisions. The clinically oriented manager is seen as an ideal, a person who is able to incorporate the world of science into the world of action.

The Academic Orientation. Academically oriented managers are high utilizers of scientific information but are rather insensitive to social and political realities. They are often highly regarded in their academic or professional disciplines and tend to emphasize the internal logic of an issue. Caplan concludes that these managers use scientific information in modest amounts and in routine ways.

The Advocacy Orientation. Managers in this category are immersed in the world of action, and their use of scientific information is almost always subordinate to the demands of social and political constraints. Any information that does

* This entire discussion of managerial orientations is paraphrased from the University of Michigan Institute for Social Research *Newsletter* (Spring 1974) Volume II, Number 1. The Study was conducted by Nathan Caplan, who is Acting Director of the Center for Research on the Utilization of Scientific Knowledge.

not support the position being advocated is apt to be ignored.

Until there are some very fundamental changes in the curricula of graduate and professional schools or the methods of recruiting managers in human service organizations, there seems little likelihood of solving either of these problems. What is possible, however, is to utilize the revolutionary advances in information processing to change the ways in which managers receive and process information and thus change the ways managers use information.

FROM DATA TO INFORMATION TO AUTOMATION. One of the consequences of having multiple data generating subunits, overlapping but specialized, is that a manager may be faced with contradictory conclusions. In the ordinary course of events, such a situation is salutary because it increases a manager's options and broadens his perspectives. In crisis situations, however, it may result in data overload and bring to the foreground any festering competition among subunits vying for scarce resources, including managerial attention. What is required, from the manager's point of view, is the conversion of data into information. The word *data* is the plural of *datum,* meaning fact. The word *information* refers to data that has been processed to achieve a purpose or enhance understanding [10:4].* One solution is to automate the various sources of data or information, thus making them readily available to

---

* The authors are fully aware that these definitions are the exact opposite of those suggested in the scientific literature where data is defined as information that is configured and processed in such a way as to permit conclusions. In this discussion we are adhering to the lexicon of the designers of management information systems.

managers. The major advantages of automated information systems usually cited are the speed of their operation and the quantity of information that can be handled. For the human service organization manager, however, the major advantage is likely to be in the word *system,* or the integration of data elements into usable information.

FROM AUTOMATION TO ACCOUNTABILITY AND INTEGRATION.

The demand for the public accountability of public programs has increased faster than the ability of managers to respond. Despite impressive advances in the evaluation of programs, evaluative capabilities have increased arithmetically, while demands for accountability have increased geometrically. As Elpers and Chapman note:

> The time has passed, if it ever existed, when those responsible for delivering human services are given sizable sums of money to spend in any desired way. Accountability encompasses far more than simply the demand for careful accounting procedures to show that public funds are not absconded. Not only are providers asked to show that services are reaching large numbers of people but also that services are having a meaningful impact on their lives. [11:1–3]

The increasing demands for accountability and the increasing complexities of management both require vast quantities of high-quality information which is clear, timely, reliable, valid, adequate, and wide-ranging [12]. A technologically feasible solution is the integration of information from various sources into a unified automated system.

Although the movement towards developing and implementing information systems is rapidly accelerating, there are many definitions and interpretations about what constitutes an information system. The name *Management Information System* is especially popular because it implies that the information produced by such a system is to be used by managers. A global definition of the MIS is provided by Walter Kennevan:

> A management information system is an organized method of providing past, present, and projection information relating to internal operations and external intelligence. It supports the planning, control and operational functions of an organization by furnishing uniform information in the proper timeframe to assist the decision-making process. [13:63]

Sanders defines management information systems as "networks of data processing procedures developed in the organization, *and integrated as necessary,* for the purpose of providing managers with timely and effective decision-making information" [10:63].

Whatever the variations, the definitions suggest that a MIS is an organized method of gathering, processing, condensing, and filtering data until it becomes relevant, reliable, timely, and accurate information for use in decision making. It intends to provide a *total* information package, but what is total will depend upon the size of the organization and the information managers want, need, and can afford.

Program evaluation becomes one element of such a system—to the extent that it can be routinized. Ideally, information concerning the worth of programs, in terms of the impacts on clients, other programs, and the general population, is collected and processed as routinely as, for instance, information on collections and disbursements. Such routinization would reduce—but not eliminate—many of the methodological problems discussed in Chapters 3 and 4 and would reduce some resistances. With the incorporation of evaluation, the MIS becomes a continuous monitoring system (see Chapters 2 and 3) with all of the advantages of time-series designs and few problems of reliability. Such routinization permits the evaluator to devote more of his energies to the exercise of his analytic skills, thus optimizing his utility to the manager.

SOME NOTES OF CAUTION. The promise of automated management information systems is great, and indeed they could well be the panacea that evaluators are claiming. There is some danger, however, of the disappointment of inflated expectations. We should note that at the time of this writing no management information system actually in operation even includes, much less integrates, program evaluation; so as yet the MIS as a continuous monitoring technique is promising but undemonstrated. The current interest on the part of the National Institutes is their second wave of enthusiasm. During the late 1950s and 1960s several large-scale multi-year MIS efforts were funded. One general conclusion from that experience was that they did not address evaluation, and managers tended not to use the systems, although they were of some utility to researchers.

Indeed, one of the problems that no amount of design can solve is the ability and inclination of managers to use the systems or to incorporate evaluation information into their decisions. Even when outcome information is routinely available, managers are slow to use it. In one preliminary study, evaluation data was rated as having more importance to management decisions than pressures from funding sources, but less than staff input, staff capability, clinical judgment and personal experience, consumer input, requirements of official policy and direct orders, and supervisors' opinions and pressures [3:70]. In short, the development of more sophisticated information systems is a necessary but not sufficient condition to improved management.

Incorporating evaluation into the design of an MIS is difficult mostly because outcome and impact data are of a different order than most routinely recorded in service organizations. If an MIS is to fulfill its promise as an evaluation mechanism, a concern for the design of an MIS must be matched by a concern with establishing the mechanisms and structures necessary to secure the constituent data elements.

Most management information systems are based on the assumption that the information needs of managers at all levels can be satisfied from a single data base. While there are good inferential and theoretical reasons for such an assumption, it remains to be verified. No one argues that all managers need the same information, only that the differences are more in scope and generality than in nature and kind. Figure 6.2, which is adapted from Head [14], presents schematically how such a system might work.

Managers at the top level are concerned with the efficiency, effectiveness, and quality of programs to justify resource requirements and expenditures in terms of the quality and appropriateness of the services rendered for the clients' needs [15:326]. Middle-level managers are accountable for the implementation of policies within the constraints of available resources. Managers at the operat-

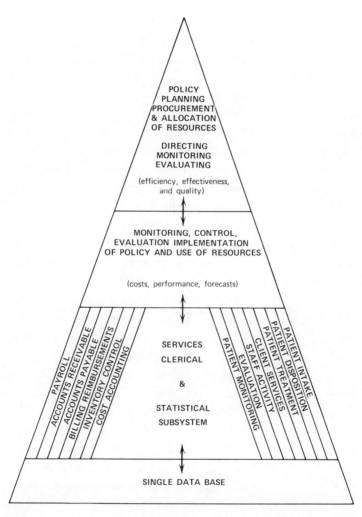

Figure 6.2. Management information system—an organized method of gathering, processing, condensing, and filtering data until they become relevant, reliable, timely, and accurate *information* for use in decision-making.

ing level require a great deal of detailed information about day-to-day activities, but only for a single program. A single data base means that all managers have information of equal reliability and validity, differing only in form and the extent to which it has been condensed and filtered. Figure 6.2 describes the internal information system—activities within the organization. As one moves up the management structure, the requirements for external information increase. For this and other reasons, it remains to be seen how adequately the information needs at all levels of management can be met by a single data-base system.

Glaser [6] warned that one of the dangers of routinizing evaluation through propositional inventories is rigidity. Rigidity is many times more a problem when routinizing evaluation by incorporation into an MIS. Very little evaluation data is currently capable of being routinized into an MIS, and that which can be routinized is, at best, rudimentary. Any kind of closure would be dangerously premature. There is a real danger, however, that the very act of routinization will have the effect of rigidifying evaluation efforts and technology. For this and other reasons, the already developed evaluation structures must be maintained into the foreseeable future, even as an organization moves toward routinization. An organization probably cannot successfully incorporate evaluation into an MIS until program evaluation as a formal specialized activity has been clearly identified and firmly consolidated.

THE FUTURE.   Although cost and technological constraints may slow the movement toward the development and implementation of management information systems, the concept of an integrated information system for decision makers is likely to have a profound impact on program evaluation in large service organizations. Because program evaluation alone among the data-generating organizational subunits claims to provide conclusions about programs in terms of results, we can reasonably expect that evaluation subunits will have an important role in integrating and organizing data from all organizational subunits into comprehensive monitoring and evaluation systems. To the extent that this happens, program evaluation will approach its potential as a management tool.

Both of the mechanisms of routinization discussed here are likely to be prominent in the future of program evaluation, but it is essential that they proceed together—"under the same umbrella," so to speak. At this point in the emergence of program evaluation as a subspecialty, specialization would only retard and perhaps reverse the precarious synthesis that gives the activity its unique identity.

REFERENCES

1. Peter F. Drucker, "Managing the Public Service Institution," *The Public Interest*, XXX, 43–60 (Fall 1973).
2. Daniel J. Levinson and Gerald Klerman, "The Clinician-Executive," *Psychiatry*, XXX, 3–25 (1967).
3. Douglas Bigelow, "The Impact of Therapeutic Effectiveness Data on Community Mental Health Center Management: The Systems Evaluation Project," *Community Mental Health Journal*, XI, 64–73 (#1, 1975).
4. David F. Musto, "Whatever Happened to Community Mental Health?" *The Public Interest*, XXXIX, 53–79 (Spring 1975).
5. The Comptroller General of the United States, *Need For More Effective Management of Community Mental Health Centers Program*, Report to Congress, August 27, 1974.

6. Daniel Glaser, *Routinizing Evaluation: Getting Feedback of Effectiveness of Crime and Delinquency Programs,* DHEW Publication No. (HSM) 73-9123, 1973.

7. Joseph Wholey, et al., *Federal Evaluation Policy,* The Urban Institute, Washington, D.C., 1971.

8. Lawrence E. Lynn, Jr., "A Federal Evaluation Office?" *Evaluation,* I, 57 (#1, 1973).

9. Paul McCullough, "Training for Evaluators—Overview," Paper presented at the National Conference on Evaluation in Alcohol, Drug Abuse and Mental Health Programs, Washington, D.C., April 1–4, 1974.

10. Donald H. Sanders, *Computers and Management in a Changing Society,* McGraw-Hill, New York, 1970.

11. Richard J. Elpers and Robert Chapman, *Design for a Countywide Computer-Based Statistical Information System,* Santa Ana, Calif.: Orange County Department of Mental Health, 1973.

12. Harold Wilensky, *Organizational Intelligence: Knowledge and Policy in Government and Industry,* Basic Books, New York, 1967.

13. Walter Kennevan, "MIS Universe," *Data Management* (September 1970).

14. Robert Head, "Management Information Systems: A Critical Appraisal," *Datamation* (May 1967).

15. Earl S. Pollak, Charles D. Windle and Cecil Wurster, "Psychiatric Information Systems: An Historical Perspective," in J. L. Crawford, D. W. Morgan, and D. T. Gianturco (eds.), *Progress in Mental Health Information Systems,* Ballinger, Cambridge, Mass.

Epilogue

This book has outlined the development and current state and status of program evaluation as a management subspecialty. Some of the most frequently used methods for the conduct of evaluation have been presented. The aim has been primarily to instruct students and practitioners about the field and its present and potential applications. The history of evaluation has resembled disorganized combat far more than it has resembled the orderly unfolding of a colorful blossom. In this epilogue we use our experiences and observations to attempt some "crystal ball gazing" into the future of program evaluation.

To anticipate our conclusions, the major problems in evaluation are not so much methodological difficulties as those of the organizational settings in which evaluation must operate. The methodological difficulties are admittedly great. The final maturation of program evaluation rests to no small extent upon the development of new methodologies, especially in the areas of multivariate analysis, epidemiology, and social indicators. On the other hand, increasing sophistication in the applications of computer technology will facilitate solution to some of the other methodological problems. Without underrating the difficulty and importance of these methodological problems, we think that these problems are solvable in the foreseeable future, and represent the less problematic of the issues facing program evaluation in the management of social programs. At the very least, it can be said that methodological difficulties are not likely to contribute significantly to retarding the development and acceptance of evaluation.

The organizational contexts of program evaluation, however, have seriously hindered its development and incorporation into management structures and processes. The most common cause of this lies in the training of those who administer most human service programs. Most administrators come to their jobs with little or no training or background in management. They tend to be practitioners who exemplify the old observation that if a person is good enough at what he does, he can stop doing it and go into administration. Furthermore, many professional training programs have tended to downgrade administration to the level of a second-rate, barely honest activity. The result has been administrators with little knowledge of evaluation, less ability to use its information, and a certain embarrassment about identifying as managers at all. Almost inevitably, evaluation has been seen as a luxury, clearly secondary to direct services, as well as a threat in exposing the possible shortcomings of managers. Only rarely was good management thought of as integrally necessary to good service delivery, even though many of these managers were directing very large and complex organizations. As a result of such sometimes massive resistances, based we feel on inadequate preparation for managerial roles, evaluation has been used in limited, sometimes inappropriate, and sometimes self-defeating ways.

For instance evaluation has been used as a tool of public relations. By suppressing evaluations that might be construed as unflattering, managers use information to justify and extol their programs. Although such an application of evaluation is appropriate, the selectivity is not—it precludes the positive uses of negative evaluations in the areas of program improvement and political advantage.

Evaluation has also been utilized to support decisions already made, as noted in earlier chapters. This is also an indication of strong resistance to true evaluation, since it requires the dismissal of any evidence or information suggesting a different decision. Information collected for the sole purpose of supporting a decision already made, even if it is called evaluation, can hardly be expected to enhance and clarify the intended purpose of evaluating programs.

It is our feeling that this situation will continue to prevail for some time. Managers continue to be chosen from the ranks of practitioners, and the avoidance of possible embarrassment is ubiquitous. However, the "crystal ball" definitely indicates that the situation is changing, and will continue to do so. The most prominent and encouraging sign of change is that the curricula of professional schools increasingly are including administration, sometimes to the point of identified specialties. This move must eventually result in greater acceptability of administration as a professional role and in evaluation as an integral part of that role. Hospital administration and education administration have probably moved the farthest in this direction, but other professions are following. In addition, bodies of evidence are developing that permit practitioners to learn "the wisdom of more modest expectations"—hence to have more realistic expectations of the results of their efforts and, hopefully, be less easily embarrassed and less resistant to the efforts of evaluation. In sum, organizational and managerial resistances to evaluation will continue for the foreseeable future but they are changing and should continue to change at an accelerating rate.

Another retardant to the development of evaluation, a feature of the organizational setting, involves the time perspective necessary to optimize the contribution of program evaluation. Program evaluation is basically a long term investment. In most instances, evaluation is introduced into ongoing programs, which were not planned and implemented with a prior notion of careful evaluation. Those programs that included systematic evaluation in their planning usually require a fairly long period of time for their results to be demonstrable. Coupled with this is the rather short tenure of human service program managers. Whether publicly or privately funded and elective or appointive in nature, the management of service organizations is a high risk occupation—most studies seem to indicate that five years or less is the average. Under these circumstances few managers will be willing and able to project the long view and make the investment necessary to incorporate ongoing evaluation, whose benefits the manager will probably not realize. The result has been a tendency to use evaluation (or what is called evaluation) as an arm of the manager, rather than as an arm of management. The most obvious solution to this problem would be to depoliticize the jobs of top managers. Certainly, the professional and popular literature is full of such pleas, whether the position is publicly or privately funded. Some kind of tenure arrangement for managers is certainly conceivable, but, in our opinion, the current trend is for managerial positions to become more, not less, political. Eventually such trends will become self-defeating, and, pendulum-like, reverse themselves but not soon.

A result of the effects of the short time perspective of most managers, and their poor preparation for incorporating evaluation into their management styles, evaluation functions tend to be centralized. This has the possibly laudable effect of placing evaluation at the most stable portion of the organization, and the questionable effect of moving evaluation further from the point of program decisions. Illustrative of this tendency is the increasing power of legislative staffs (state and federal), and federal laws that dictate the federal development of evaluation requirements. In all public and private agencies there is a tendency to locate the responsibility for evaluation at the policy, rather than at the programmatic level. We predict that this tendency will be short lived, because of a contravailing tendency to place increasing accountability at the level of the manager. One likely and commendable outcome of these conflicting tendencies will be a clearer delineation of program evaluation and policy analysis—that is, a distinction between what is apt to happen and what does happen.

The role of the federal government in the future of program evaluation deserves some special predictions. All

types and levels of programs are increasingly dependent on
federal funds for their continuation and/or expansion, and
few question the right of those entrusted with public tax
revenues to place constraints on what those revenues are to
accomplish. From the perspective of program evaluation,
three trends require attention.

1. *Standardization.* Many of the newer federal laws require
   the establishment of minimal standards for service delivery, if the program is to qualify for federal support. We
   are not concerned here with the shortcomings or the advantages of federally determined standards (the shortcomings arise from the diversity of the country, the advantages from the universal protection of the public), but
   only with the effect that the establishment of standards
   will have on evaluation. Wherever standards are
   developed (in fact, the closer to the program, the more
   stringent the standards seem to be) they will not and cannot pass for long as evaluations. Standards, at best, can
   describe the conditions without which a program cannot
   be effective (in the opinions of those who set standards),
   but can never describe those conditions that will ensure
   effectiveness. Such insurance cannot be delivered in the
   foreseeable future. Therefore, evaluation will test the
   standards, not the other way around, and the demands for
   accountability will soon separate the standards from the
   evaluation.
2. *Continuous monitoring.* The federal government will
   provide the inpetus, but not the direction for the incorporation of evaluation into continuous monitoring
   systems. The federal government is currently in its
   second wave of enthusiasm for management information
   systems. Realizing that its first flush of enthusiasm did
   not result in its promised solution to the problems of
   evaluation, however, the government in its most recent
   legislation (at least in mental health and developmental

disabilities) separates the admitted advantages of management information systems from the equally necessary requirements of program evaluation. Prediction: sophisticated computer technology, demands for accoutability, and additional requirements that evaluation be a recognized part of management will result in the incorporation of evaluation into management information systems. After some delay, the resources necessary to do it will be found.

3. *The specification of evaluation requirements.* The skepticism of legislators and the advances in evaluation technology (probably in that order) have led to federal legislation requiring outcome evaluation. In this, the agents of the federal government are meeting enormous resistance, stemming from causes already mentioned. Prediction: outcome evaluation will become a federal requirement and will be incorporated into the managerial activities of administrators, but only with great reluctance, and only after several battles (perhaps in court) about the abilities of programs to comply. What are apt to be the federal requirements will not tax the technology of evaluation.

Other trends, more in the national culture than in the administration of its programs, will profoundly influence the role of program evaluation. The fabric of "the American Dream" is changing. Most social and human service programs, spawned in political arenas, lack measurable goals and clear linkages between goals and program activities. At best these programs intend to impact on social problems and human conditions for which acceptable solutions are unknown. Political designers and the general public believed that, given sufficient funding and manpower, programs could change almost every social problem and human condition. Predicated on the premise that human behavior is infinitely malleable, social programs were and, to a lesser extent, still are designed to change people. As long as deviant human behavior is considered the symptom rather than a cause of a social problem and so long as human behavior is assumed to be extremely pliable, intervention, albeit naive, at the public level is assumed to be justified. If, however, human behavior is assumed to be genetically or biologically determined, what then is to be the intervention?

It is becoming increasingly apparent that present assumptions may be inaccurate and the expensive intervention approaches usually do not work. Demands for accountability, including requests for specifications of program goals and expected results of program activities, are pointing out glaringly inefficient and ineffective programs. A growing body of literature provides some evidence for the increased public awareness that programs generally fail to do what they purport to do.

The long range potential is not easily estimated, but fewer illusions, widespread realism, and eroded faith in the "American Dream" affect and are affected by this new awareness.

Mixed with additional demands for accountability resulting from economic pressures, the effect of this awareness is likely to be profound. Prediction: evaluation is to become more visible and more often demanded by funding agencies. More federal and state resources will be allocated for evaluation.

Bibliography

GENERAL INTEREST

Adams, R., and J. Preiss, eds. *Human Organization Research,* Dorsey Press, Homewood, Ill., 1960.

American Institute of Research, *Evaluative Research, Strategies and Methods,* Pittsburg, Pa., 1970.

Attkisson, C. Clifford, et al., *A Workingpeoples Guide to the Community Mental Health Program Evaluation Literature,* The Program Evaluation Project, Department of Psychiatry, University of California, San Francisco, 1973.

Bernstein, Ilene, and Howard E. Freeman, *Academic and Entrepreneurial Research: The Consequences of Diversity in Federal Evaluation Studies,* Russell Sage Foundation, New York, 1975.

Binderman, Albert, and Laure Sharp, "The Evaluation Research Community: RFP Readers, Bidders and Winners," *Evaluation,* II, 36–40 (#1, 1974).

Blau, P., "Formal Organizations-Dimensions of Analysis," *American Journal of Sociology,* LXIII, 58–69 (July 1957).

Buchanan, Garth, and Joseph Wholey, "Federal Level Evaluation," *Evaluation,* I, 17–22 (#1, 1972).

Caro, Francis G., "Integration of Evaluative Research and Social Planning Roles: A Case Study," *Human Organization,* XXXIII, 351–358 (#4, 1974).

Caro, Francis G., *Readings in Evaluation Research,* Russell Sage Foundation, New York, 1971.

Carter, G., "The Challenge of Accountability-How We Measure the Outcomes of our Efforts," *Public Welfare,* XXIX, 267–277 (Summer 1971).

Carter, Reginald, "Clients' Resistance to Negative Findings and the Latent Conservative Function of Evaluation Studies," *The American Sociologist,* VI, 118–124 (May 1971).

Chafetz, Morris, "Monitoring and Evaluation at NIAAA," *Evaluation,* II, 49–52 (#1).

Chatterjee, Pranab, "Decision-Support System: A Case Study in Evaluative Research," *The Journal of Applied Behavioral Science,* XI, 62–74 (#1, 1975).

Davis, Howard R., "Insights—A Solution for Crisis?" *Evaluation,* I, 3–5 (#1, 1972).

Etzioni, Amatai, *Modern Organizations,* Prentice-Hall, Englewood Cliffs, N.J., 1964.

Fleck, A. C., "Evaluation as a Logical Process," *Canadian Journal of Public Health,* LII, 185–191 (1961).

Flint, Robert T., "Evaluation: The Key to Better Police Service?" *Evaluation,* I, 6–8 (#1, 1972).

Garn, Harvey A., and Mancur Olson, "Human Services on the Assembly Line," *Evaluation* I, 36–42 (#2, 1973).

Glaser, Daniel "Remedies for the Key Deficiency in Criminal Justice Evaluation Research," *Research in Crime and Delinquency,* 144–154 (July 1974).

Glaser, Daniel, *Routinizing Evaluation: Getting Feedback on Effectiveness of Crime and Delinquency Programs,* National Institute of Mental Health, Washington, D.C., DHEW Publication No. (HSM)73–9123.

Granof, Michael and Charles Smith, "Accounting and the Evaluation of Social Programs: A Comment," *The Accounting Review,* XLIX, 822–826 (October, 1974). Reply by E. L. Sobel and M. E. Francis, pp. 926–830.

Gutek, Barbara, et al., "Utilization and Evaluation of Government Services by the American People," *Evaluation,* II, 41–48 (#1, 1974).

Guttentag, Marcia, "Models and Methods in Evaluation Research," *Journal for the Theory of Social Behavior,* I, 75–97 (#1, 1971).

Guttentag, Marcia, "Subjectivity and Its Uses in Evaluation Research," *Evaluation,* I, 60–65 (#2, 1973).

Hage, J., and M. Aiken, *Social Change in Complex Organizations,* Random House, New York, 1970.

Hargreaves, William, et al., eds., *Resource Materials for Community*

Mental Health Program Evaluation, National Institute of Mental Health, Washington, D.C., 5 volumes, no date.

Hatry, Harry P., R. E. Winnie, and D. M. Fish, *Practical Program Evaluation for State and Local Government Officials,* The Urban Institute, Washington, D.C., 1973.

Herzog, E., *Some Guidelines for Evaluative Research,* U.S. Department of Health, Education and Welfare, Social Security Administration, Children's Bureau, Washington, D.C., 1959.

Hetherington, Robert, et al., "The Nature of Program Evaluation in Mental Health," *Evaluation,* II, 78–82 (#1, 1974).

Hutchinson, George B., "Evaluation of Preventive Services," *Journal of Chronic Diseases,* XI, 497–508 (May 1960).

Institute on Rehabilitation Services, *Program Evaluation: A Beginning Statement,* U.S. Department of Health, Education and Welfare, Rehabilitation Services Administration, Washington, D.C., 1972.

King, Larry, et al., "Accountability, Like Charity, Begins at Home," *Evaluation,* II, 75–77 (#1, 1974).

Kunce, J. T., and C. S. Cope, *Rehabilitation and the Culturally Disadvantaged,* Research Series I, Part III, University of Missouri, Columbia, 1969.

Larkin, E. J., *The Treatment of Alcoholism: Theory, Practice and Evaluation,* Adddiction Research Foundation of Ontario, Ontario, 1974.

Larsen, Judith, and Darly Nichols, "If Nobody Knows You've Done It, Have You . . . ?" *Evaluation,* I, 39–44 (#1, 1972).

Laska, Eugene, et al., "The Multi-State Information System," *Evaluation,* I, 66–71 (#1, 1972).

Lennard, Henry L., and Arnold Bernstein, "Dilemma in Mental Health Program Evaluation," *American Psychologist,* undated reprint.

Levine, A. S., "Evaluating Program Effectiveness and Efficiency," *Welfare in Review,* 1–7 (February/March 1970).

Levine, Adeline, and Murray Levine, "Evaluation Research in Mental Health: Some Lessons From History," paper presented at the National Conference on Evaluation in Alcohol, Drug Abuse and Mental Health Programs, Washington, D.C., April 1974, mimeo.

Lewis, Frank L., and Frank G. Zarb, "Federal Program Evaluation from the OMB Perspective," *Public Administration Review,* XXXIC, 308–317 (July/August 1974).

Lynn, Laurence E., Jr., "A Federal Evaluation Office?" *Evaluation,* I, 56–59 (#2, 1973).

Mangum, G. L., and L. M. Glenn, *Vocational Rehabilitation and Federal*

Manpower Policy, U.S. Government Printing Office, Washington, D.C., 1967.

McCullough, Paul, "Training for Evaluators—Overview," paper presented at the National Conference of Evaluation in Alcohol, Drug Abuse and Mental Health Programs, Washington, D.C., April 1–4, 1974.

Mondale, Walter F., "Social Accounting, Evaluation, and the Future of the Human Services," *Evaluation,* I, 29–34 (31, 1972).

National Advisory Council on Education Professions Development, *Search for Success: Toward Policy on Educational Evaluation,* Washington, D.C., June 1974.

National Institute of Mental Health, *Planning for Creative Change in Mental Health Services: Use of Program Evaluation,* (HSM 71-9057), Washington, D.C., no date.

Poland, Orville, "Program Evaluation," *Public Administration Review,* XXXIV, 299–330 (July/August 1974).

Reissman, "A Study of Role Conception in Bureaucracy," *Social Forces,* XXVII, 305–310 (1949).

Riedel, Donald, Gary Tischler, and Jerome K. Myers, eds., *Patient Care Evaluation in Mental Health Programs,* Ballinger, Cambridge, Mass., 1974.

Rivilin, A. M., *Systematic Thinking for Social Action,* The Brookings Institute, Washington, D.C., 1971.

Rossi, Peter H., and Walter Williams, eds., *Evaluating Social Programs,* Seminar Press, New York, 1962.

Salasin, Susan, "Setting Program Priorities for People: Evaluating Environmental Programs," *Evaluation,* I, 14–16 (#3, 1973).

Salasin, Susan, "Exploring Goal-Free Evaluation: An Interview with Michael Scriven," *Evaluation,* II, 9–16 (#1, 1974).

Schick, A., "From Analysis to Evaluation," *The Annals,* CCCLXIV, 57–71 (March 1971).

Schulberg, Herbert, Alan Sheldon, and Frank Baker, *Program Evaluation in the Health Fields,* Behavioral Publications, New York, 1969.

Southard, Curtis G., *Symposium on the Evaluation of Community Mental Programs,* National Institute of Mental Health, Washington, D.C., 1952–53.

Southern Regional Educational Board, *Definition of Terms in Mental Health, Alcohol Abuse, Drug Abuse, and Mental Retardation,* Mental Health Statistics Series #8, National Institute of Mental Health, Washington, D.C.

Spencer, G., *Structure and Dynamics of Social Intervention,* Northeastern

University Studies in Rehabilitation, #9, Heath Lexington Books, Lexington, Mass., 1970.

Staats, Elmer, "The Challenge of Evaluating Federal Social Programs," *Evaluation*, I, 50–54 (#3, 1973).

Stockdill, James W., "The Politics of Program Evaluation," paper presented at the 14th Annual Conference of the Department of Mental Health and Mental Retardation of the Commonwealth of Virginia, November 1974.

Suchman, Edward, *Evaluative Research,* Russell Sage Foundation, New York, 1967.

Sundquist, J. L., ed., *Perspectives on Fighting Poverty,* Basic Books, New York, 1969.

Trantow, D., "An Introduction to Evaluation: Program Effectiveness and Community Needs," *Rehabilitation Literature,* XXXI, ˙ 2–9 (January 1970).

Tripodi, Tony, Irwin Epstein, and Carol MacMurray, "Dilemmas in Evaluation: Implications for Administrators of Social Programs," *American Journal of Orthopsychiatry,* XL, 850–854 (October 1970).

Tripodi, Tony, Phillip Fellin, and Irwin Epstein, *Social Program Evaluation: Guidelines for Health, Education and Welfare Administrators,* F. E. Peacock Publishers, Itasca, Ill., 1971.

Walker, Robert A., "The Ninth Panacea: Program Evaluation," *Evaluation,* I, 45–53 (#1, 1972).

Weiss, Carol H., *Evaluating Action Programs: Readings in Social Action and Education,* Allyn & Bacon, Boston, 1972.

Weiss, Carol H., *Evaluation Research,* Prentice-Hall, Englewood Cliffs, N.J., 1972.

Weiss, Carol H., "Between the Cup and the Lip," *Evaluation,* I, 49–55 (#2, 1973).

Whitaker, Gordon, "Who Puts the Value in Evaluation," *Social Science Quarterly,* 759–761 (March 1974).

Wholey, Joseph S., John W. Scanlon, Hugh G. Duffy, James S. Fukumoto, and Leona M. Vogt, *Federal Evaluation Policy,* The Urban Institute, Washington, D.C., 1970.

Williams, Richard and Lucy D. Ozarin, eds., *Community Mental Health: An International Perspective,* Jossey-Bass, San Francisco, 1968.

Wilner, Daniel, et al., "Databank of Program Evaluations," *Evaluation,* 3–6 (#3, 1973).

Wilner, D. M., "Evaluation: The State of the Technical Art," paper presented at the National Conference on Evaluation in Alcohol, Drug

Abuse and Mental Health Programs, Washington, D.C., April 1974, mimeo.

Zusman, Jack, and Murray Levine, *International Journal of Mental Health,* II, entire issue (Summer 1973).

Zusman, Jack, and Eleanor Ross, "Evaluation of the Quality of Mental Health Services," *Archives of General Psychiatry,* XX, 352–(March 1969).

METHODS

American Psychological Association, *Standards for Educational and Psychological Tests and Manuals,* Washington, D.C., 1966.

Bateman, W., "Assessing Program Effectiveness—A Rating System for Identifying Relative Project Success," *Welfare in Review,* VI, 1–10 (January 1968).

Blalock, Hubert M., Jr., *Social Statistics,* McGraw Hill, New York, 1960.

Blum, Henrik, "Evaluating Health Care," *Medical Care,* XII, 999–1011 (December 1974).

Boruch, R. F., "Problems in Research Utilization: Use of Social Experiments, Experimental Results and Auxiliary Data in Experiments," *Annals of the New York Academy of Sciences,* 1973.

Burton, T. L., and G. E. Cherry, *Social Research Techniques for Planners,* Allen and Unwin, London, 1970.

Campbell, Donald T., and Julian C. Stanley, *Experimental and Quasi-Experimental Designs for Research,* Rand McNally, Chicago, 1966.

Campbell, Donald T., "Reforms as Experiments," *American Psychologist,* XXIV, 409–429 (April 1969).

Ciocco, A., "On Indices for the Appraisal of Health Department Activities," *Journal of Chronic Diseases,* XI, 509–522 (1961).

Cochran, W. C., *Sampling Techniques,* Wiley, New York, 1963.

Cornfield, J., and W. Haenszel, "Some Aspects of Retrospective Studies," *Journal of Chronic Diseases,* X (January/June 1960).

Cronback, L., "Coefficient Alpha and the Internal Structure of Tests," *Psychometrika,* XVI, 297–334 (1951).

Cronback, L., and P. Mechl, "Construct Validity of Psychological Tests," *Psychological Bulletin,* LII, 281–302 (1955).

Cronback, L., *Essentials of Psychological Testing,* 2nd ed., Harper & Row, New York, 1960.

Dalkey, Norman C., *Delphi,* P-3704, (October 1967), Rand Corporation, Santa Monica, Calif.

Davis, James A., *Elementary Survey Analysis,* Prentice-Hall, Englewood Cliffs, N.J., 1971.

Davis, R. V., et al., "Methodological Problems in Rehabilitation Research," *Minnesota Studies in Vocational Rehabilitation,* University of Minnesota, Bulletin 24.

Deniston, O. L., I. M. Rosenstock, and V. A. Getting, "Evaluation of Program Effectiveness," *Public Health Reports,* LXXXIII, 323–335 (April 1968).

Deniston, O. L., et al., "Evaluation of Program Efficiency," *Public Health Reports,* LXXXIII, 603–610 (July 1968).

Donabedian, A., "Evaluating the Quality of Medical Care," *Millbank Memorial Quarterly,* XLIV, 166–203 (July 1966).

Donabedian, A., *A Guide to Medical Care Administration, Vol. II, Medical Care Appraisal Quality and Utilization,* The American Public Health Association, Washington, D.C. 1969.

Durkheim, Emile, *The Rules of Sociological Method,* Free Press, New York, 1938.

Fine, J. S., "A Systems Approach to Manpower Utilization," Working Paper #1, National Study of Social Welfare and Rehabilitation Workers, Work and Organizational Contexts, U.S. Dept. of Health, Education and Welfare, 15–30 (May 1971).

Glaser, Edward M., and Thomas Backer, "A Clinical Approach to Program Evaluation," *Evaluation,* I, 54–60 (#1, 1972).

Glaser, Edward M., and Thomas Backer, "A Look at Participant Observation," *Evaluation,* I, 46–49 (#3, 1973).

Gogsted, A., *Evaluation of Factors Determining the Results of Vocational Rehabilitation,* Williams and Wilkins, Baltimore, 1968.

Goodstadt, Michael, ed., *Research on Methods and Programs of Drug Education,* Ontario, Addiction Research Foundation of Ontario, 1974.

Gordon, R. L., *Interviewing, Strategy, Techniques and Tactics,* Dorsey Press, Homewood, Ill., 1969.

Greenberg, B. G., "Evaluation of Social Programs," *Review of the International Statistical Institute,* XXXVI (#3, 1968).

Guilford, J., *Psychometric Methods,* McGraw-Hill, New York, 1954.

Hefferin, E. A. and E. Katz, "Issues and Orientations in the Evaluation of Rehabilitation Programs: A Review Article," *Rehabilitation Literature,* XXXII, 93–113 (April 1971).

Hinrichs, H. H., and G. M. Taylor, *Systematic Analysis: A Primer on Benefit-Cost Analysis and Program Evaluation,* Goodyear Publishing Co., Pacific Palasades, Calif., 1972.

Horvitz, D. G., "Methodological Considerations in Evaluating the Effectiveness of Programs and Benefits," *Inquiry,* II, 96–104 (1965).

Kerlinger, Fred N., *Foundations of Behavioral Research,* Rinehard and Winston, Inc., New York, 1964.

Kessner, D., and C. Kalk, *A Strategy for Evaluating Health Services,* Institute of Medicine, National Academy of Sciences, Washington, D.C., 1973.

Light, R. J., F. Mosteller, and H. S. Winokur, Jr., "Using Controlled Field Studies to Improve Public Policy," *Federal Statistics: Report of the President's Commission,* U.S. Government Printing Office, Washington, D.C., 367–402, 1971.

Lindquist, E., ed., *Educational Measurement,* American Council on Education, Washington, D.C., 1951.

MacMahon, B., T. F. Pugh, and J. Ipsen, *Epidemiologic Methods,* Little, Brown and Co., Boston, 1960.

Macmillan, A. M., "The Health Opinion Survey Technique for Estimating Prevalence of Psychoneurotic and Related Types of Disorder In Communities," Monograph Supplement #7, *Psychological Reports,* III, 325–339 (September 1957).

Madge, John, *The Tools of Social Science,* Doubleday, New York, 1965.

Mahoney, T., A. Annoni, and G. Milkovich, "The Use of the Delphi Technique in Manpower Forecasting," *Management Science,* XIX (December 1972).

Miller, Delbert C., "The Shaping of Research Design in Large-Scale Group Research," *Social Forces,* XXXIII, 383–390 (May 1955).

Miller, D., *Handbook of Research Design and Social Measurement,* David McKay, New York, 1964.

Mosteller, F., and D. P. Moynihan, eds., *On Equality of Educational Opportunity,* Random House, New York, 1972.

Oppenheim, A. N., *Questionnaire Design and Attitude Measurement,* Basic Books, New York, 1966.

O'Toole, R., ed., *The Organization, Management and Tactics of Social Research,* Schenkman Publishing Co., Cambridge, Mass., 1971.

Roos, Noralou, "Contrasting Social Experimentation with Retrospective Evaluation: A Health Care Perspective," *Public Policy,* XXIII, 241–257 (Spring 1975).

Rosen, Beatrice M., *A Model for Estimating Mental Health Needs Using 1970 Census Socioeconomic Data,* National Institute of Mental Health, Series C, #9.

Rosenstock, I., "Some Principles of Research Design in Public Health," *American Journal of Public Health,* LI (February 1951).

Salasin, Susan, "Experimentation Revisited: A Conversation with Donald Campbell," *Evaluation,* I, 7–13 (#3, 1973).

Selltiz, Claire, et al., eds., *Research Methods In Social Relations,* Rinehart and Winston, New York, 1967.

Sheps, M. C., "Approaches to Quality of Hospital Care," *Public Health Reports,* LXX, 877–886 (September 1955).

Siegle, S., *Non Parametric Statistics,* McGraw-Hill, New York, 1956.

Sjoberg, Gideon, and Roger Nett, *A Methodology for Social Research,* Harper & Row, New York, 1968.

Skutsch, M. and J. Schofer, "Goal Delphis for Urban Planning and Concepts in Their Design," *Socio-Economic Planning Science,* VII, 305–313 (1973).

Stevens, S. S., "On the Theory of Scales and Measurement," *Science,* 684, 677–680 (June 7, 1946).

Stouffer, Samuel H., "Some Observations on Study Design," *American Journal of Sociology,* LV, 355–361 (1950).

Thompson, Charles, and Gustav Rath, "The Administrative Experiment: A Special Case of Field Testing or Evaluation," *Human Factors,* XVI, 238–252 (June 1974).

Tousignant, Michel, and Guy Denis, "Psychiatric Patients and the 'Untreated' Cases of Epidemiological Surveys: A Comparative Analysis of the Self-Concept," *Social Science & Medicine,* IX, 39–42 (1975).

Webb, E. J., Donald Campbell, Richard Schwartz, and Lee Sechrest, *Unobtrusive Measures: Nonreactive Research in the Social Services,* Rand McNally, Chicago, 1966.

Wigner, E. P., ed., *Physical Science and Human Values,* Princeton University Press, Princeton, N. J., 1947.

Williams, Walter, "The Capacity of Social Science Organizations to Perform Large-Scale Evaluative Research," Public Policy Paper #2, Institute of Government, University of Washington, 1971.

MODELS AND APPROACHES—TYPOLOGIES

Academy of Management Journal, XV, entire issue (December 1972).

Attkisson, C. Clifford, et al., "A Working Model for Mental Health Program Evaluation," *American Journal of Orthopsychiatry,* XLIV, 741–753 (October 1974).

Barnsby, S., *Cost-Benefit Analysis and Manpower Programs,* D. C. Heath, Lexington, Mass., 1972.

Beightler, Charles S., and Velna Rae Thurman, "Management Science Models for Evaluating Regional Government Policies," *Omega,* III, 71–78 (#1, 1975).

Borus, M., "A Benefit-Cost Analysis of the Economic Effectiveness of Retraining Unemployed," *Yale Economic Essays,* 1964.

Burgess, John, Ronald Nelson, and Robert Walhaus, "Network Analysis as a

Method for the Evaluation of Service Delivery Systems," *Community Mental Health Journal,* X, 337–344 (#3, 1974).

Caro, Francis G., "Approaches to Evaluation Research: A Review," *Human Organization,* XXVIII, 87–99 (#2, Summer 1969).

Churchman, C. West, *The Systems Approach,* Dell, New York, 1968.

Edwards, Ward, "Social Utilities," *The Engineering Economist,* Summer Symposium Series, VI (1971).

Etzioni, Amitai, "Two Approaches to Organizational Analysis: A Critique and a Suggestion," *Administrative Science Quarterly,* V, 257–278 (September 1960).

Etzioni, Amitai, "Public Policy: In Perspective," *Evaluation,* I, 23 (#1, 1972).

Etzioni, Amitai, "Alternative Conceptions of Accountability," *Hospital Progress,* 34–59 (June 1974).

Henriot, Peter, *Political Aspects of Social Indicators: Implications for Research,* Russell Sage Foundation, New York, 1972.

James, George, "Evaluation and Planning of Health Programs," *Administration of Community Health Services,* International City Managers Association, Chicago, 125–218, 1961.

Key Factor Analysis Workbook, Jarett, Rader and Longhurst, Raleigh, N.C., 1970.

Kiresuk, Thomas J., "Goal Attainment Scaling: A General Method for Evaluating Comprehensive Community Mental Health Programs," *Community Mental Health Journal,* IV, 443–453 (1968).

Otis, Todd, "Measuring 'Quality of Life' in Urban Areas," *Evaluation,* I, 35–38 (#1, 1972).

President's Panel on Social Indicators, *Toward a Social Report,* U.S. Government Printing Office, Washington, D.C., 1969.

Scanlon, J. W., *An Evaluation System to Support Planning Allocation and Control in a Decentralized, Comprehensive Manpower Program,* The Urban Institute, Washington, D.C., 1971.

Schulberg, H., and F. Baker, "Program Evaluation Models and the Implementation of Research Findings," *American Journal of Public Health,* LVIII (September 1968).

Seashore, S. E., "Criteria of Organizational Effectiveness," *Michigan Business Review,* XVII, 26–30 (July 1965).

Starfield, Barbara, "Measurement of Outcome: A Proposed Scheme," *Milbank Memorial Fund Quarterly,* 39–50 (Winter 1974).

Stein, H. D., M. Houghman, and S. R. Zalba, "Assessing Social Agency Effectiveness: A Goal Model," *Welfare In Review* (March/April 1968).

Tyler, Ralph W., et al., *Perspectives of Curriculum Evaluation,* AERA

Monograph Series on Curriculum Evaluation, No. 1, Rand McNally, Chicago, 1967.

Weiss, Carol H., "Alternative Models of Program Evaluation," *Social Work,* XIX, 675–681 (November 1974).

Western Interstate Commission for Higher Education, *Systems Approach to Program Evaluation in Mental Health,* Boulder, Colo., 1970.

Wilcox, Leslie, et al., *Social Indicators and Societal Monitoring,* Josey Bass, San Francisco, 1972.

Wilson, J. O., "Social Experiments and Public Policy Analysis," *Public Policy,* XXII, 15–38 (Winter 1974).

STATE-OF-THE-ART

Adams, Stuart, "Evaluative Research in Corrections: Status and Prospects," *Federal Probation,* XXXVIII, 14–21 (March 1974).

Argyris, Chris, "Creating Effective Research Relationships in Organizations," *Human Organizations,* XVII, 34–40 (#1, 1958).

Argyris, Chris, *The Applicability of Organizational Sociology,* Cambridge University Press, Cambridge, 1972.

Brown, L. Dave, "Research Action: Organizational Feedback, Understanding, and Change," *The Journal of Applied Behavioral Science,* VIII, 697–711 (#6, 1972).

Buchanan, Garth, Pamela Horst, and John Scanlon, "Improving Federal Evaluation Planning," *Evaluation,* I, 86–90 (#2, 1973).

Coleman, James, *Policy Research in the Social Sciences,* General Learning Corporation, Morristown, N.J., 1972.

Davis, Howard R., "Four Ways to Goal Attainment: An Overview," *Evaluation,* I, 43–49 (#2, 1973).

Eidell, Terry L., and Joanne M. Kitchel, eds., *Knowledge Production and Utilization in Educational Administration,* Center for the Advanced Study of Educational Administration, Eugene, Oregon, 1968.

Engelsmann, F., H. B. M. Murphy, and F. C. Tcheng-Laroche, "Criteria for the Post-Hospital Adjustment of Mental Patients in Sheltered Settings," *Canadian Psychiatric Association Journal,* XIX, 375–380 (1974).

Feldman, Saul, "Community Mental Health Centers: A Decade Later," *International Journal of Mental Health,* III, 19–34 (#2–3, 1974).

Gonnella, Joseph and Carter Zeleznik, "Factors Involved in Comprehensive Patient Care Evaluation," *Medical Care,* XII, 928–934 (November 1974).

Greenberg, B. G. and B. F. Mattison, "The Whys and Wherefores of

Program Evaluation," *Canadian Journal of Public Health,* XLVI (July 1955).

Harris, Darrel, and Timothy Brown, "Relationship of the Community Adaptation Schedule and the Personal Orientation Inventory: Two Measures of Positive Mental Health," *Community Mental Health Journal,* X, 111–118 (#1, 1974).

Klerman, Gerald, "Current Evaluation Research on Mental Health Services," *American Journal of Psychiatry,* CXXXI, 783–787 (July 1974).

Kornhauser, William, *Scientists in Industry,* University of California Press, Berkeley, 1961.

Lewicki, Roy J., and Clayton Alderfer, "The Tensions Between Research and Intervention in Intergroup Conflict," *The Journal of Applied Behavioral Science,* IX, 423–468 (#4, 1973).

Maruyama, Magoroh, "Endogenous Research vs. 'Experts' From Outside," *Futures,* 389–394 (October 1974).

Mazer, M., "People in Predicament: A Study in Psychiatric and Psychosocial Epidemiology," *Social Psychiatry,* XI, 85–90 (1974).

Mitchell, Terence R., "An Interview Study Points Out the Problem with 'Contract' Evaluation," *Evaluation,* I, 21–23 (#2, 1973).

Mushkin, Selma J., "Evaluation: Use with Caution," *Evaluation,* I, 31–35 (#2, 1973).

Nelson, Ronald, "Accountants 1, Psychologists 0," paper presented at the National Conference on Evaluation in Alcohol, Drug Abuse and Mental Health Programs, Washington, D.C., April 1974.

Smith, R. C., "Program Evaluation: Any Prime Sponsor Can," *Manpower,* VII, 2–6 (#5, 1975).

Sussman, Marvin B., ed., *Sociology and Rehabilitation,* American Sociological Association, Washington, D.C., 1965.

Weiss, Carol H., "Where Politics and Evaluation Research Meet," *Evaluation,* I, 37–45 (#3, 1973).

Wessen, A. F., "On the Scope and Methodology of Research in Public Health Practice, *Social Science and Medicine,* VI, 469–490 (1972).

Westheimer, Ruth, "Evaluation Criteria and Psychotherapy Research," *Psychotherapy and Psychosomatics,* XXV, 236–238 (1975).

Wholey, Joseph, and Bayla While, "Evaluation's Impact on Title I Elementary and Secondary Education Program Management," *Evaluation,* I, 73–76 (#3, 1973).

Williams, Walter, and John Evans, "The Politics of Evaluation: The Case of Headstart," *The Annals,* CCLXXXV, 118–132 (September 1969).

Wortman, Paul, "Evaluation Research: A Psychological Perspective," *American Psychologist,* XXX, 562–574 (May 1975).

EXAMPLES

Abbott, Ronald C., and Barbara Frank, "A Follow-Up of LD Children in a Private School," *Academic Therapy*, X, 291–297 (Spring 1975).

Adamson, John, Robert Fostakowsky, and Farouk S. Chebib, "Measures Associated with Outcome on One Year Follow-up of Male Alcoholics," *British Journal of Addiction*, LXIX, 325–337 (1974).

Angrist, Shirley S., Mark Lefton, Simon Dinitz and Benjamin Pasamanick, *Women After Treatment: A Study of Former Mental Patients and Their Normal Neighbors*, Appleton Century-Crofts, New York, 1968.

Aron, William S., and Douglas Daily, "Short and Long Term Therapeutic Communities: A Follow-Up and Cost Effectiveness Comparison," *International Journal of Addictions*, IX, 619–636 (#5, 1974).

Beck, Dorothy Fahs, "Research Findings on the Outcome of Marital Counseling," *Social Casework*, 153–181 (March 1975).

Becker, Marshall, Robert Drachman, and John Kirscht, "A Field Experiment to Evaluate Various Outcomes of Continuity of Physician Care," *American Journal of Public Health*, LXIV, 1062–1070 (November 1974).

Bolin, David C., and Laurence Kivens, "Evaluation in a Community Mental Health Center: Huntsville, Alabama," *Evaluation*, II, 26–35 (#1, 1974).

Botein, B., "The Manhattan Bail Bond Experiment," *Texas Law Review*, XLIII, 319–331 (1965).

Chervany, Norman, and Gary Dickson, *An Experimental Evaluation of Information Overload in a Production Environment*, Management Information Systems Research Center Working Paper Series, University of Minnesota, Minneapolis, 1972.

Ciarlo, James A., et al., "A Multi-Dimensional Outcome Measure for Evaluating Mental Health Programs," mimeo.

Ciarlo, James A., "A Performance-Monitoring Approach to Mental Health Program Evaluation," (January 1972) mimeo.

Coleman, J. S., E. Q. Campbell, C. F. Hobson, J. McPartland, A. M. Mood, et al., *Equality of Educational Opportunity*, U.S. Government Printing Office, Washington, D.C., 1966.

Coleman, J. S., *The Evaluation of Equality of Educational Opportunity*, Report No. 25, Center for the Study of the Social Organization of Schools, Johns Hopkins University, Baltimore, Md., 1968.

Coolidge, John C., and Richard Brodie, "Observations of Mothers of 49 School Phobic Children: Evaluated in a 10 Year Follow-Up Study," *Journal of Child Psychiatry*, XIII, 275–285 (Spring 1974).

Davis, Ann, Simon Dinitz, and Benjamin Pasamanick, "The Prevention of Hospitalization in Schizophrenia: Five years After an Experimental

Program," *American Journal of Orthopsychiatry,* 42(3), 375–388 (April 1972).

Dinitz, Simon, "Policy Implications of an Experimental Study in the Home Care of Schizophrenia," *Sociological Focus,* I, 1–19 (#2, Winter 1967).

Doherty, Gillian, "On-Going Program Effectiveness Evaluation in a Token Economy," *Canadian Journal of Behavioral Science,* VII 97–103 (#2, 1975).

D'Orban, P. T., "A Followup Study of Female Narcotic Addicts: Variables Related to Outcome," *The British Journal of Psychiatry,* CXXV, 28–33 (July 1974).

Gearing, Frances Rowe, "Methadone Maintenance Treatment Five Years Later—Where Are They Now," *American Journal of Public Health Supplement,* LXIV, 44–50 (December 1974).

Gillies, Marion, et al., "Outcomes in Treated Alcoholics," *Journal of Alcoholism,* IX, 125–134 (#4, 1975).

Glick, Ira, William Hargreaves, and Michael Goldfield, "Short vs. Long Hospitalization," *Archives of General Psychiatry,* XXX, 363–369 (March 1974).

Gottschalk, Louis, Ruth Fox, and Daniel Bates, "A Study of Prediction and Outcome in a Mental Health Crisis Clinic," *American Journal of Psychiatry,* CXXX, 1107–1111 (October 1973).

Hackler, James, and John Hagan, "Work and Teaching Machines as Delinquency Tools: A Four-Year Follow-Up," *The Social Science Review,* LXIX, 92–106 (March 1975).

Hawk, Alan, William Carpenter, and John Strauss, "Diagnostic Criteria and Five-Year Outcome in Schizophrenia," *Archives of General Psychiatry,* XXXII, 343–347 (March 1975).

Herrera, Elizabeth, Betty Glasser Lifson, Ernest Hartmann, and Maida Solomon, "A 10-Year Followup of 55 Hospitalized Adolescents," *American Journal of Psychiatry,* CXXXI, 769–774 (July 1974).

Jones, Fredric, "A 4-Year Follow-Up of Vulnerable Adolescents," *The Journal of Nervous and Mental Disease,* CLIX, 20–39 (#1, 1974).

Katz, Daniel and Naphtali Golomb, "Integration, Effectiveness and Adaptation in Social Systems: A Comparative Analysis of Kibbutzim Communities," *Administration and Society,* VI, 399–421 (February 1975).

Kiresuk, Thomas J., "Goal Attainment Scaling at a County Mental Health Service," *Evaluation,* Special Monograph #1, 12–18.

Kivowitz, Julian, Judith Forgotson, Gerald Goldstein and Fred Gottlieb, "A Follow-Up Study of Hospitalized Adolescents," *Comprehensive Psychiatry,* XV, 35–42 (January/February 1974).

Lotter, Victor, "Social Adjustment and Placement of Autistic Children in

Middlesex: A Follow-Up Study," *Journal of Autism and Childhood Schizophrenia,* IV, 11–32 (#1, 1974).

Melotte, Christopher, and Alan Ogborne, "Strategies for the Successful Follow-Up of Treated Drug Users," *Journal of Drug Issues,* 79–82 (Winter 1975).

Morris, Joann S., and Fred Ebrahimi, *American Indian Alcoholism Evaluation-Monitoring-Design project. Final Report,* Tribal American/Training Consultants Associated, Glendale, Calif. 1974.

Mosher, Loren, Alma Menn, and Susan M. Mathews, "Soteria: Evaluation of a Home-Based Treatment for Schizophrenia," *American Journal of Orthopsychiatry,* XLV, 455–467 (April 1975).

Ohlin, Lloyd E., Robert Coates, and Alden Miller, "Evaluating the Reform of Youth Correction in Massachusetts," *Journal of Research in Crime and Delinquency,* 3–16 (January 1975).

Pasamanick, Benjamin, Frank Scarpitti, and Simon Dinitz, *Schizophrenics in the Community: An Experiment in the Prevention of Hospitalization,* Appleton-Century-Crofts, New York, 1967.

Price, J. L., "A Study of Organizational Effectiveness," *Sociological Quarterly,* XIII, 3–15 (#1, 1972).

Pusser, H. Ellison, and Boyd McCandless, "Socialization Dimensions Among Inner-City Five-Year-Olds and Later School Success: A Follow-Up," *Journal of Educational Psychology,* LXVI, 285–290 (#3, 1974).

Quinn, Patricia, and Judity Rapoport, "One-Year Follow-Up of Hyperactive Boys Treated with Imipramine or Methylphenidate," *American Journal of Psychiatry,* 132, 241–245 (March 1975).

Robin, Gerald, "The In-School Neighborhood Youth Corps Program," *Evaluation,* II, 53–57 (#1, 1974).

Romond, Anne, Catherine Forrest, and Herbert Kleber, "Follow-Up of Participants in a Drug Dependence Therapeutic Community," *Archives of General Psychiatry,* XXXII, 369–374 (March 1975).

Scheer, Nancy, and Gail Barton, "A Comparison of Patients Discharged Against Medical Advice with a Matched Control Group," *American Journal of Psychiatry,* CXXXI, 1217–1220 (November 1974).

Skipper, James K., Jr., and Charles H. McCaghy, "Evaluation of a Short-Term Treatment Program for Police Case Inebriates," *Social Science,* XLIX, 220–227 (#4, 1974).

Skoloda, Thomas, et al., "Treatment Outcome in a Drinking-Decisions Program," *Journal of Studies on Alcohol,* XXXVI, 365–380 (#3, March 1975).

Smith, William, "Evaluation of the Clinical Services of a Regional Mental Health Center," *Community Mental Health Journal,* XI, 45–57 (#1, 1975).

Stein, Leonard, Joseph Newton, and Richard Bowman, "Duration of Hospitalization for Alcoholism," *Archives of General Psychiatry,* XXXII, 247–252 (February 1975).

Stromsdorfer, E. W., *Review and Synthesis of Cost-Effectiveness Studies of Vocational and Technical Education,* ERIC Clearinghouse on Vocational and Technical Education, Ohio State University, (1972).

Towle, Leland, et al., *Alcoholism Program Monitoring System Development—Evaluation of the ATC Program,* (HSM-42-71-115), Stanford Research Institute, March 1973.

Williams, George, Fu-tong Hsu and Tsung-yi Lin, "Prediction of the Burden of Released Mental Patients," *Community Mental Health Journal,* IX, 303–315 (#4, 1973).

EVALUATION AND MANAGEMENT

Bigelow, Douglas A., "The Impact of Therapeutic Effectiveness Data on Community Mental Health Management: The Systems Evaluation Project," *Community Mental Health Journal,* XI, 64–73 (#1, 1975).

Brown, Richard, and Ray D. Pethtel, "A Matter of Facts: State Legislative Performance Auditing," *Public Administration Review,* XXXIV, 318–327 (July/August 1974).

Crawford, Jeffrey L., D. W. Morgan, and D. T. Gianturco, *Progress in Mental Health Information Systems,* Ballinger, Cambridge, Mass., 1974.

Drucker, Peter F., "Managing the Public Service Institution," *Public Interest,* XXX, 43–60 (Fall 1973).

Drucker, Peter, *Practice of Management,* Harpers, New York, 1955.

Elpers, Richard and Robert Chapman, *Design for A Countywide Computer Based Statistical Information System,* Orange County Department of Mental Health, Santa Ana, Calif., 1973.

Feldman, Saul, "Problems and Prospects: Administration in Mental Health," *Administration in Mental Health,* National Institute of Mental Health, 4–11 (Winter 1972).

Guttentag, Marcia, and Kurt Snapper, "Plans, Evaluations, and Decisions," *Evaluation,* II, 58–64 (#1, 1974).

Head, Robert, "Management Information Systems: A Critical Appraisal," *Datamation* (May 1967).

Horst, Pamela, Joe N. Nay, John Scanlon, and Joseph S. Wholey, "Program Management and the Federal Evaluator," *Public Administration Review,* XXXIV, 300–308 (July/August 1974).

Johnson, R., F. Kast, and J. Rosenzweig, *The Theory and Management of Systems*, McGraw Hill, New York, 1963.

Kennevan, Walter, "MIS Universe," *Data Management* (September 1970).

Marvin, Keith E. and James L. Hedrick, "GAO Helps Congress Evaluate Programs," *Public Administration Review*, XXXIV, 327–333 (July/August 1974).

McGregor, Douglas, "An Uneasy Look at Performance Appraisal," *Harvard Business Review*, XXXV (May–June 1957).

Mohr, Lawrence B., "The Concept of Organizational Goal," *The American Political Science Review*, LXVII, 470–471 (June 1973).

Morehouse, Thomas A., "Program Evaluation: Social Research Versus Public Policy," *Public Administration Review*, XXXII (November/December 1972).

Musto, David F., "Whatever Happened to 'Community Mental Health'?" *The Public Interest*, XXXIX, 53–79 (Spring 1975).

Poland, Orville, "Program Evaluation and Administrative Theory," *Public Administration Review*, XXXIV, 333–338 (July/August 1974).

Sanders, Donald, *Computers and Management In a Changing Society*, McGraw-Hill, New York, 1970.

Schultz, C. L., *The Politics and Economics of Public Spending*, The Brookings Institution, Washington, D.C., 1969.

Whyte, William, and Edith Hamilton, *Action Research for Management*, Dorsey Press, Homewood, Ill., 1964.

Wilensky, Harold, *Organizational Intelligence: Knowledge and Policy in Government and Industry*, Basic Books, New York, 1967.

RELATED

Ackoff, R., and M. W. Sasieni, *Fundamentals of Operations Research*, Wiley, New York, 1968.

Balinsky, Warren, and Renee Berger, "A Review of Research on General Health Status Indicators," *Medical Care*, XIII, 283–293 (April 1975).

Berg, Ole, "Health and Quality of Life," *Acta Sociologica*, XVIII, 3–22 (#1, 1975).

Borus, M. E., and W. R. Tash, *Measuring of the Impact of Manpower Programs*, University of Michigan Institute of Labor and Industrial Relations, Ann Arbor, November, 1970.

Cho, Yong Hyo, "A Multiple Regression Model for Measurement of the

Public Policy Impact on Big City Crime," *Policy Sciences,* III, 435–455 (1972).

Delberg, A. L., and A. H. Van de Van, "A Group Process Model for Problem Identification and Program Planning," *Journal of Applied Behavioral Science,* IV, 466–492 (1971).

Edie, Leslie C., "The Quality and Maturity of Operations Research," *Operations Research,* XXI, 1024–1029 (September–October 1973).

Etzioni, Amitai, "The Next Crisis: The End of the Family?" *Evaluation,* II, 6–7 (#1, 1974).

Etzioni, Amitai, "PSRO: A New Way to Manage Our Health System?" *Evaluation,* I, 55–56 (#3, 1973).

Gifford, Bernard, "Policy Analysis and the City," *Evaluation,* I, 26–30 (#3, 1973).

Gilbert, Niel, Harry Spect, and Charlane Brown, "Demographic Correlates of Citizen Participation: An Analysis of Race, Community Size, and Citizen Influence," *The Social Service Review,* XLVIII, 517–530 (December 1974).

Halpert, Harold, William Horvath, and John P. Young, *An Administrators Handbook on the Application of Operations Research to the Management of Mental Health Systems,* U.S. Department of Health, Education and Welfare, Washington, D.C., Public Health Service Publication #2110.

Lawrence, J. R., ed., *Operational Research and the Social Sciences,* Tavistock Institute, London, 1966.

Lehne, Richard, and Donald Fisk, "The Impact of Urban Policy Analysis," *Urban Affairs Quarterly,* X, 115–138 (December 1974).

Levinson, Raniel and Gerald Klerman, "The Clinician-Executive," *Psychiatry,* XXX, 3–15 (1967).

MacRae, Duncan, Jr., "Policy Analysis as an Applied Social Science Discipline," *Administration and Society,* VI, 363–388 (February 1975).

Mannins, Fortune, and M. F. Shore, *Consultation Research in Mental Health and Related Fields,* Public Health Monograph #79, Public Health Service Publication #2122, U.S. Department of Health, Education and Welfare, U.S. Government Printing Office, Washington, D.C., 1971.

Martin, David B., and Carole Parsons, "A Code of Fair Information Practice for Statistical-Reporting and Research Operations," *Evaluation,* I, 31–36 (#3, 1973).

McLean, Peter, and James Miles, "Evaluation and the Problem-Oriented Record in Psychiatry," *Archives of General Psychiatry,* XXXI, 622, 625 (November 1974).

Mitroff, Ian, and Louis Pondy, "On the Organization of Inquiry: A Comparison of Some Radically Different Approaches to Policy Analysis," *Public Administration Review,* XXXIV, 471–479 (September 1974).

Shevsky, Eshref, and Marilyn Williams, *The Social Areas of Los Angeles,* University of California Press, Berkeley, 1949.

Shevsky, Eshref and Wendell Bell, *Social Area Analysis,* Stanford University Press, Palo Alto, 1955.

Tomkins, Richard, "Evaluating National Health Insurance Legislation: A Summary Review," *Hospital Administration,* XIX, 74–84 (Summer 1974).

Warheit, George, Roger A. Bell, and John J. Schwab, *Planning for Change: Needs Assessment Approaches,* The National Institute of Mental Health, Washington, D.C., no date.

OTHER

Brim, Orville, and Stanton Wheeler, *Socialization After Childhood,* Wiley, New York, 1966.

Farris, R. E. L., and H. W. Dunham, *Mental Disorders in Urban Areas,* University of Chicago Press, Chicago, 1939.

Hammond, John L., "Two Sources of Error in Ecological Correlations," *American Sociological Review,* XXXVIII, 764–777 (December 1973).

Hollingshead, A. B., and F. C. Redlich, *Social Class and Mental Illness: A Community Study,* Wiley, New York, 1958.

Levinson, Daniel J., and Eugene Gallagher, *Patienthood in the Mental Hospital,* Houghton Mifflin, Boston, 1964.

Parsons, Talcott, *The Social System,* Free Press, Glencoe, Ill., 1951.

Robinson, W. S., "Ecological Correlation and the Behavior of Individuals," *American Sociological Review,* XV, 351–357 (June 1950).

Thrasher, Jean H., and Harvey L. Smith, "Interactional Contexts of Psychiatric Patients: Social Roles and Organizational Implications," *Psychiatry,* XXVII, 389–398 (November 1964).

Index

229